Yoga at Your Wall

Stretch Your Body,
Strengthen Your Soul,
Support Your Practice

Stephanie Pappas
Author of **Yoga Posture Adjustments and Assisting**

Trafford
PUBLISHING

Order this book online at www.trafford.com/08-0251
or email orders@trafford.com

Most Trafford titles are also available at major online book retailers.

Stephanie Pappas
42 Elm Street
Somerset, NJ, 08873, USA
stefanipappas@hotmail.com

Photographic models (photos used with permission):
Stephanie Pappas, Kim Karsh, Pauline Gyllenhammer, Paula Pablo, Jacqueline Olsen, Charlotte Avallone, Silvia Revuelta, Erin Kipe-Klemme, Laura Rodriguez, Manuel Cano Diaz, Maria Guadalupe Diaz Alcantara.

Photos with fish painting shot on location at the beach in Tulum, Mexico at Zamas Hotel and Que Fresco Restaurant; www.Zamas.com

Book photographs by:
Stephanie Pappas, Carrie Haley, Manuel Cano Diaz, and the photographic models

Editor: Martha D. Humphreys; www.CoachWrite.com
Contributing editors: Grinning Moon Creative; www.GrinningMoon.com, Sue Jorgenson

Book cover design: Stephanie Pappas and Trafford Publishing designers
Book interior design and layout: Grinning Moon Creative; www.GrinningMoon.com

Note for Librarians: A cataloguing record for this book is available from Library and Archives Canada at www.collectionscanada.ca/amicus/index-e.html

ISBN: 978-1-4251-7213-8

We at Trafford believe that it is the responsibility of us all, as both individuals and corporations, to make choices that are environmentally and socially sound. You, in turn, are supporting this responsible conduct each time you purchase a Trafford book, or make use of our publishing services. To find out how you are helping, please visit www.trafford.com/responsiblepublishing.html

Our mission is to efficiently provide the world's finest, most comprehensive book publishing service, enabling every author to experience success. To find out how to publish your book, your way, and have it available worldwide, visit us online at www.trafford.com/10510

 www.trafford.com

North America & international
toll-free: 1 888 232 4444 (USA & Canada)
phone: 250 383 6864 ♦ fax: 250 383 6804 ♦ email: info@trafford.com

The United Kingdom & Europe
phone: +44 (0)1865 487 395 ♦ local rate: 0845 230 9601
facsimile: +44 (0)1865 481 507 ♦ email: info.uk@trafford.com

10 9 8 7 6 5 4 3 2

Dedication

To my parents, June and Dean, who continue to love and encourage me through whatever life delivers. To my friend Carrie Haley whose compassion and support helped get me through the walls I hit while I wrote this book.

To my recent Devalila yoga teacher trainees who kept me inspired while I wrote this book: Katherine Standley, Eadaoin O'Donovan, Kim Karsh, Pauline Gyllenhammer, Jackqueline Olsen, Paula Pablo, and Charlotte Avallone.

To my cats for sitting on my lap and offering me comfort when it was hard to write.

To my yoga and meditation teachers who are gracious enough to share their love and wisdom with me

Contents

A Letter from the Author

Dear Readers,

No coincidences.

During the past year as I wrote Yoga at Your Wall, I experienced one of the most challenging years of my life. As I practiced yoga at physical walls in NJ and Mexico, I also found myself against emotional walls, intellectual walls, and spiritual walls. So many distractions interfered with my writing. At times, what appeared to be stumbling blocks between me and completing this book were actually starting blocks motivating me to write more. Writing and yoga, yoga and writing became the safe places to be.

I offer this book to you in gratitude for getting me through a challenging year. If you find yourself against the wall, hitting your wall, or between a wall and a hard place in life, know that you are not alone. As you read these pages, keep in mind that I was encountering the largest and hardest walls in my life.

At the beginning, I had no electricity in the Caribbean cabin I call home. To order to keep writing, I relied on electrical outlets at friend's homes and internet cafes. I wrestled with menopausal symptoms, allergies, and various tropical diseases which were all exaggerated by the intense summer heat and humidity. I swatted away a variety of tropical pests between paragraphs: scorpions, spiders, mosquitoes, flies, ants and another unidentified insect that bit in its own unique way. I scratched and itched during file saves.

A few weeks after the initial concept for this book began taking shape, my mom was rushed to the hospital in New Jersey. The diagnosis was heart failure. I shuttled myself back and forth between NJ and Mexico all year. And then there was the break-up of a very intense 6 year relationship, and learning to live alone in a foreign country.

Eventually I had electricity, but so did my neighbors. As I powered up my computer, they powered up their stereo and celebrated with thunderous music and around the clock parties—some lasting for 4 days. As the walls vibrated around me, I inserted my ear plugs and wrote more.

Practicing yoga is an act of kindness toward ourselves. Even if we dedicate 10 minutes a day to our own well-being, self-awareness, and spirit in the middle of chaos and drama, it is time well spent.

I hope this book inspires you to practice more yoga— wherever and whenever you encounter walls!

Namaste,
Stephanie Pappas
Thanksgiving Day 2008

Introduction

"Practice makes the heart grow fonder."

– Stephanie Pappas

Why practice yoga at your wall?

What walls do for us: they provide structure, containment, safety, shelter, limitations, support, and definition. As an aid in your yoga practice, a wall helps you articulate precise alignment and form in each pose, supports you when you want to relax, assists you when you want to try a new posture, and motivates you to more fully energize your body.

A wall is your teacher when there is no human teacher around to guide or adjust you in a yoga posture.

"I thought yoga at the wall would be wimpy, but it was really challenging!" said Eadaoin, one of my advanced yoga teacher trainees, after taking one of my yoga wall classes. Her comment ignited my enthusiasm to write this book.

And after experiencing the legs-up-the-wall restorative relaxation pose, Charlotte said, "I have never felt so relaxed in my whole life!"

Some accuse the wall of being a crutch; how unfair to both you and the wall! In my experience the wall feels like a trusty friend, one who always tells me the truth, whether I want to hear it or not. Until becoming friends with your wall, when you practice yoga postures you have only the floor — a horizontal reference point — to know where your body is in space.

When practicing at the wall, you have a vertical reference point for your further orientation. You can lean on it, align yourself with it, push off of it, or press into it. The wall not only assists you, it adds another degree of challenge to your practice.

When you leave the wall and go back to practicing on the floor, you have a whole new level of awareness of your alignment and a different experience of your body. You may visit the wall more often than you can imagine. Through this practice, I became "one with my wall."

Doing yoga at your wall is logical, portable, and practical. Have you ever wanted to lie on the floor and stretch in your hotel room while you were on a trip, but the floor just didn't look all that clean or appealing? It's a perfect time to practice your wall yoga.

Or maybe you're dressed in a suit or a dress, ready for a meeting or presentation, and feeling a little stressed. You want to do some yoga, but you know you will wrinkle clothes if you get on the floor. It's yet another perfect opportunity to find your nearest yoga wall.

The benefits of practicing yoga vertically serve you well at home, at your office, and anywhere there is a wall to befriend.

Join me on our journey to expand the possibilities of your yoga practice.

When you "hit your wall"

You may have had times when it seems like a slew of problems find you all at once, or just one immensely painful thing happens. Or maybe you keep encountering one small annoying problem over and over again. You hit an emotional, mental, or physical wall and think, "I just can't go through this!" The wall you hit may be in your relationships, work, interactions with people, or interaction with yourself. Your heart and mind may consciously or unconsciously shut down. Life is certainly ripe with opportunities to shut down, isn't it?

At times like these you may stop doing what you love, or what is good for you —including your yoga practice. I am not going to tell you that yoga posture practice will always help you break through the tough times, or that by practicing yoga you won't hit as many walls in your life, but I am going to tell you that your yoga practice will ease the transition from emotional, mental, or physical discomfort to acceptance.

Yes, there were times when I've practiced, and I've felt more centered and balanced. There were times when I hit a wall and didn't practice at all; I just laid in bed and cried. Sometimes we just plain old freak out and lose our presence of mind. There were times when I wanted so badly not to feel what I was feeling, and times when I felt every feeling in my body 100 percent.

If you are new to yoga, I am telling you this because I want to paint a realistic picture for you. If you are an experienced practitioner, I am telling you this because I want to remind you not to lay guilt trips on yourself for not practicing as much as you may think you should. Sometimes you may just want to sit still and breathe, and go no further. At other times you may want to push through your perceived limitations and break your patterns.

So, if you feel like you are hitting a wall in life, you can practice yoga— or not. I am not going to tell you that you must practice yoga at these times, or that yoga is the only solution for when you hit your wall. No guilt, no regrets. I am going to tell you though that it is a step toward acceptance of the situation. There are other possibilities available to you when you hit your wall: call a friend, see a counselor, healer, or life coach, cry your eyes out, go to sleep, write in your journal, dress up and take yourself out to dinner, or take a day trip to some place you have never been. Do something different to break the pattern and lighten up if possible.

*Whatever it is you choose to do when you hit your wall, you can also **soften** toward yourself while you're doing it.*

How to use this book

Please do more than just read this book.

Use it, interact with it, look at the pictures for clarification, note the pointers and most of all, learn and enjoy this alternative to floor practice. My book is designed for you to practice yoga, not just read about it. The pictures with pointers and side notes will help you understand and incorporate the pose quickly while you are practicing at your wall. I imagine you pressing the book open and laying it on the floor to experiment with the postures. If I could have built a little portable reading lamp into the book, I would have.

The first step is to find your friend, your wall. Some students tell me their walls are full of pictures, posters, plants, and other things; others tell me they don't want to mess up their walls. Well, maybe it is time for a spring cleaning, or some rearranging. You can also find an outside wall to use if weather permits, or a sturdy door to practice on; just make sure no one will be opening the door during your practice! Once you find your piece of yoga wall you can paint symbols or decorations on it to make it more appealing to you as a place of refuge and solace.

There are five main sections of this book following this introduction. Sections 2-5 are collections of postures that are grouped together according their purpose and focus:

- Section 1 covers the essentials of practicing yoga and yoga at your wall, with alignment principles, tips, and some philosophy.

- Section 2 contains postures that primarily develop strength and increase energy including a daily flowing sequence.

- Section 3 contains postures that primarily promote a greater sense of balance and steadiness.

- Section 4 contains postures that primarily encourage stretching and flexibility.

• Section 5 contains postures that primarily support relaxation, rest, and rejuvenation.

Actually, each yoga pose offers you a little bit of everything—strength, stretching and support—depending on **how** you practice it. Perhaps you will choose to combine postures from the four different sections, or maybe you will practice a series of poses from the same section. The practice you choose depends on the time of day that you practice, your state of mind, your physical state, and your daily needs and desires.

I included a flowing posture sequence at the end of section 2 for strength to encourage you to learn to link poses together ("vinyasa" in Sanskrit), and develop your own personal practice ("sadhana" in Sanskrit).

After you have cultivated a level of comfort with each of the poses individually, you may be inspired to make up your own posture sequences. I included "create your own yoga wall sequence" worksheets at the end of each section so that you can invent and write down your own flowing sequences.

Devalila Yoga Style

"Devalila Yoga" is the name I chose to capture my personal experience with yoga and philosophy. In Sanskrit "Devalila" means the divine play of life. The name should give you a clue about my orientation toward the yoga practice.

Approach your practice with the intention to explore, play, experiment, adapt, and modify. Even if you think that you aren't physically or mentally flexible, you can learn to cultivate flexibility through your yoga practice. You will be amazed at the improvement in your well being with daily practice and your new best friend, the wall.

To get the most out of your practice, follow these basic Devalila Yoga principles:

1. Breathe deeply and consciously.

2. Feel the subtle sensations in your body.

3. Gently refocus your mind when it begins to wander.

4. Attempt to let go of criticism or judgments about yourself and your body.

5. Release any competition with anyone or anything else, including yourself.

Even with all this yoga posture information at your fingertips, it is only by practicing that you will receive full knowledge and true understanding. Remember to give your body enough time to integrate each pose that you do at the wall.

Many years ago I asked my teacher from India how yoga postures should be practiced. I expected a lengthy and elaborate response, instead he answered, **"Like a child."**

Information given for each yoga posture

Sections 2-5 include photos and information about each individual yoga posture to do at your wall. In addition to the photos, you will find the following information for each yoga at your wall pose (with the exception of slight variations and modifications of the main pose, which will have only instructions at a glance):

Level of difficulty

The level of difficulty of each pose is relative to each individual's body and experience. Depending on the age, health, and range of motion of the person doing the pose, the pose can be easy, difficult, or challenging.

Consider three criteria when you consider the level of difficulty for each pose:

1. How long you hold the pose.

2. How you breathe during the pose.

3. How much you engage your body when performing the pose.

So, if you stand in Mountain pose for two days, please don't write to me saying that it wasn't a beginner pose! Or perhaps you had your significant other push you into a forward fold pose in spite of the extremely painful sensations in your legs, or you held the plank pose for a long time shortly after rotator cuff surgery from a tennis injury—you get the idea. Also please note that these level categories may not apply to you if you are a quick learner, or have practiced other physical disciplines such as dance, sports, or martial arts.

Beginner

Students who are new to yoga practice, or have taken a few weeks or months of yoga classes from an assortment of teachers with different disciplines may consider themselves novices. This category also applies to those who have physical challenges, which inhibit their movement.

Beginner/Intermediate

Students who have practiced yoga postures for possibly about 6 months to a year, and are sometimes conscious of their breath while doing the postures. Level 1-2 students are starting to achieve a balance between effort and relaxation during practice, and are beginning to make minor adjustments to their own alignment and form.

Intermediate

Students who have practiced yoga postures for over a year, are able to consciously direct their breath, have a basic ability to make their own alignment adjustments in a pose, and are comfortable with moderate levels of sensation and physical challenge.

Intermediate/Advanced

Students who have regularly practiced yoga postures for over 2 years and/or have the ability to focus and direct their minds and their physical bodies, are able to consciously direct their breath and awareness, are skilled at making their own alignment adjustments in a pose, are responsible for their own safety, and are comfortable with high levels of sensation and physical challenge. At this level a student may be aware of the more subtle aspects of yoga practice on energy, the spirit, and the mind.

Advanced

Students who have practiced yoga postures for over 5 years and/or have a definite ability to take physical risks and direct their minds and their physical bodies, are able to consciously direct their breath and awareness while practicing, are skilled at making their own alignment adjustments in a pose, are responsible for their own safety, and are comfortable with high levels of sensation and physical challenge. At this level a student is aware of subtle movements of energy, states of consciousness, and internal contractions (called "locks" or "bandhas" in Sanskrit).

Focus and intention

Each pose benefits a part or parts of our body, and our body's structure or function. Yoga postures also help us cultivate qualities of being and inner states of mind. At the beginning of the instructions for each posture you can read the focus or intention of that posture to help you decide if you want to practice it.

Remember that there are numerous ways you can practice an individual yoga pose that will each affect your experience of it. Therefore, the affects of practicing a posture are not limited to the information I will provide you. For example, if you do a pose that is mainly designed to increase flexibility, but instead you extend the duration and firm your muscles more intensely, you can change the focus and intention.

Instructions at a glance

So that you can begin practicing the postures, and not just reading about them, you're provided with "instructions at a glance" to get practicing as soon as possible. After reading the initial "at a glance" instructions, you can go back and read the more detailed suggestions given for each pose.

Tips for getting into the pose

When further clarification is necessary, you'll find tips to gauge your distance to the wall, how your body should contact the wall, and other pointers to enhance your experience of the wall posture.

Exiting the pose

This section contains the safe ways to exit pose. Remember that injuries can occur getting into and out of poses. Some wall postures require more detailed instructions than floor poses relative to the exit from a pose.

Yoga prop suggestions

Props support your body and enhance your experience of a yoga posture. Props also add an extra level of safety and comfort to your yoga practice. Ideas and suggestions for using yoga props are given for each pose.

Ideas for breathing in the pose

Breathing is natural; it's the first thing we do when we are born, and the very last thing we will do when we die. Don't worry about getting it right. You know how to breathe! The tricky part is remembering to breathe when we stop breathing during challenging moments in life, and in the yoga practice.

When practicing the yoga postures, the breath is just as important, if not more important, than the posture. How could this be? It only takes a few minutes of not being able to breathe to realize that it is our anchor to this world—our life sustaining force.

Pay attention to the suggestions in this section for directing your breath; you will get the most benefit from the postural experience. If you find the suggestions distracting or confusing, just forget them for now and breathe consciously, easily, continuously, and naturally.

Suggestions for visual focus

"Where the eyes go, attention flows." Where you focus your gaze in the yoga practice has an effect on your body, balance, and mental concentration. In some styles of yoga there are specific eye gazing points, called "drishti" in Sanskrit. These drishti points are not hard stares, but soft, unfocused gazing points. In other yoga styles you are advised to keep your eyes closed. Each technique has its value. These areas of the book contain ideas for focusing your eyes.

Imagery for alignment

This section offers suggestions for images that you can visualize while practicing the pose. Holding a thought or image in your mind's eye may help you more easily attain precise alignment and articulate the subtleties of the yoga posture.

"Home Play" experiments— exploring and deepening the posture

My word for homework is "Home Play." Because this practice is as alive and dynamic as you are, I'll offer you optional home play experiments to enhance your practice. Try out the suggestions with a sense of curiosity. You won't be handing anything in to be graded, and no one is watching you! So have some fun exploring your body, mind, emotions, and spirit. After all, it is you that you have to live with every moment of the day and night. You might as well get to know all of yourself.

Have you ever noticed how your dog or cat prepares their sleeping area? They knead, paw, press, roll, move about, and circle (sometimes around and around) as if checking for snakes before flopping down with a satisfied sigh.

There are so many ways that we humans also fiddle with ourselves to get more comfortable, or to experience different levels of sensation. Think about your experience of kissing, hugging, and making love. Do you stay in one position and freeze? I hope not!

Yoga postures can be approached in a way that invites a release of tension, slowly and gradually; as if you are doing a "slow dance" with yourself. With the tips I'll give you in this area, I hope to encourage you to dance your way into the posture.

Deepening and playing in the pose is an essential part of my Devalila philosophy of practice (read more in Section 1). In my beginning years of practicing yoga, I experienced times of rigidity in my postural practice. I have also seen hundreds of beginner and advanced students quietly struggle in the yoga poses as a result of holding themselves so stiffly. It seemed as if they were posing for a yoga photo. Yoga postures do not have to be practiced this way! I strongly suggest that experimentation, spontaneity, and fluidity become your foundation for deepening your yoga practice.

Once you get into a pose, remember to move around! Make micro-movements; fiddle, snuggle, undulate, sway, and wiggle your body as it assumes the form of the posture. At first it may feel awkward to get to know your body in this way. Stick with it and let the innate wisdom of your body take over.

Possible benefits and experiences of the pose

My use of the word "possible" is intentional. The benefits of yoga have not been scientifically proven…yet. Nonetheless, many studies are being conducted on the benefits of yoga, and surely positive proof will emerge to support what we yoga enthusiasts feel are the inherent advantages of practicing yoga postures (called "asanas" in Sanskrit) and breathing techniques (called "pranayama" in Sanskrit).

The benefits you can receive depend on the frequency, duration, and focus of your practice.

Anything is possible. You won't know unless you practice!

Precautions

Appropriate precautions are noted in this section if the yoga posture presents a potential risk of injury to a certain part of the body, or is contraindicated for a specific condition.

Essentials for Practicing Yoga Postures and Yoga at Your Wall

Practice makes the heart grow fonder

Anytime you practice something regularly, hopefully you improve at it. Perhaps not as quickly as you expect, but you do get better, and then you begin to develop a fondness for what you are practicing. The same holds true for the practice of yoga.

At first, yoga practice may feel challenging, difficult or strained, and may make you extremely aware of your stiffness, and your inability to release the tensions in your body and mind. If you are practicing yoga, you will inevitably feel some sensations—pleasant and unpleasant.

The word yoga in Sanskrit means "to unite or to yolk." It implies that we are seeking connection with the whole of existence and with ourselves as we are in this moment. When I hear people say, "I'm not good at yoga," I realize they are probably referring to the aspect of yoga that has to do with flexibility. I attempt to share with them how beneficial and profound it is—more than just the flexibility of our hamstrings! But I remember that experience is the best teacher, and talk only goes so far.

The good news is that self awareness is the foundation of yoga practice. We are becoming Self aware. It is a process. If yoga is a process of uniting with ourselves as we are, and the world as it is— in this moment—how can we be bad at it?

My aim in this section is to share my way of practicing yoga with you as a result of 17 years of practice. I am certainly not trying to convince you of anything. My hope is that the points that resonate with you become integrated into your practice, and bring you greater joy, expansion, freedom, and peace of mind. Take what you need, leave the rest, and revisit this section periodically on your journey.

Safety tips for practicing yoga at your wall

By their nature, walls are hard surfaces. If you are used to practicing yoga without a wall, you may have a tendency at first to collide inadvertently with the wall when you are not expecting it. In addition to the specific details given for each posture about how to set up at the wall, here are some other general safety measures to keep in mind:

- Move all furniture, pictures, lamps, hanging fixtures, and objects away from the sides, back and front of you. A safe distance from objects is at least your own height with your arms extended overhead.

- Pick a smooth, even wall surface.

- Ensure there are no nails in the wall.

- Have your yoga props nearby so you don't have to reach for them while you are in a pose. Yoga props such as yoga blocks, a strap, a pillow, and a throw blanket, will add to your experience of the practice.

- Use caution when pressing your foot against the wall. In postures like warrior 3 and half moon 2 you do not look at the wall when positioning your foot, so if you are too close to the wall, you could bang your foot during the set up.

- Practice with a yoga sticky mat adjacent to the wall to prevent slipping and create a strong foundation in the base of the pose.

- When practicing arm balances like the handstand pose, make sure the ceiling is at least as high as your height on tippy toes with your arms extended. This is especially important if you will be practicing in your basement, or in a room with low ceilings.

- Practice with a window open so that you can breathe fresh air while you practice.

General alignment points for posture practice

Although each pose has its own unique alignment and form, here are some general alignment guidelines that you can apply while practicing any pose:

- Lengthen your spine.

- Relax your jaw and facial muscles.

- Keep your knees pointing in the same general direction as your toes.

- Align your knee over your ankle when bending your knees at right angles (90 degrees).

• Avoid jutting your chin out in front of your body.

• Soften the back of the neck.

• Expand and lift your chest, but not so much that you thrust your ribs forward.

• Broaden the area from your sternum to the area above your armpit.

• Accentuate the movement of your shoulders lowering down away from your ears.

• Keep your ribs in alignment with your abdomen.

• Stay aware of your feet or whatever part of your body is touching the ground.

• Allow the area around your navel center to draw inward toward the core of your body.

• Let your tailbone drop down toward the ground.

• Keep your limbs and outer extremities active and engaged during the postures.

• Deepen and lengthen your breath.

• Let your eyes softly gaze at the suggested focal point, or allow them to close as you stay aware of sensations and feeling in your body.

• Keep your head aligned with your spine, especially in the standing poses.

Exploring the opposites in yoga practice

Start to notice the opposite forces at play in your yoga practice. Yoga practice encourages you to find a balance between:

• Being stable and being supple

• Staying grounded and feeling buoyant

• Relaxing and firming your body

- Being alert and softening your focus

- Activity and stillness

- Doing and being

- Knowing and not knowing

- Being human and being spirit

- Making an effort and being at ease

- Inhaling and exhaling

- Practicing determination and flexibility

- Being disciplined and spontaneous

- Noticing your positive and not so positive qualities

Riding the waves of your breath

There are many anatomy books that discuss the mechanics of our respiratory system and the function of our lungs and diaphragm, so I won't go into that here. I don't think I need to convince you how important your breath is to your life. We humans can go for days without water, shelter, or food, but not without our breath. Here are some suggestions for increasing your lung capacity and breath awareness during your yoga posture practice:

Nostril breathing with a light ocean sound (much like a light snoring sound) in the back of the throat (called "ujjayi" breath in Sanskrit, meaning "victorious") is recommended for practicing yoga postures, but by all means breathe through your mouth if your nose is stuffed-up! It may take you a few seconds or a few weeks to master this technique, but it is worth the effort. It has a calming effect on the nervous system and has been proven to slow down our brain waves (alpha state). Because of the slight constriction created in the back of the throat, ujjayi breath allows you to have more command over your breath during yoga posture practice.

Breathing in slowly through your nose, and out slowly through your mouth is another technique I recommend to help release tension during the practice. If you find yourself stiffening up, contracting, trying too hard, thinking too much, or feeling competitive, try breathing in through your nose and out through your mouth for a little while. If possible, return to breathing in and out solely through your nose.

"One pose or one minute a day" philosophy

A daily yoga practice could last one minute or several hours. Whenever possible, allow yourself the freedom to decide. Sometimes we may think we want to practice for only five minutes and then two hours magically fly by. If you put pressure on yourself to practice for a long time, you may never practice at all. When students or teachers tell me that they can't practice or get started practicing on their own, I suggest they try my "one pose or one minute a day" plan. They always seem so surprised when I suggest this. Give yourself a break and try just one pose a day or one minute a day at the beginning and see what happens. Let me know how it goes.

Ways to practice on your own

You have tons of options for your yoga posture practice. If you find that practicing feels like an obligation or a habit, try something new to bring some more enjoyment into it. It is possible to throw out all of your previous conceptions and create a new practice on a daily basis. What is most important is honoring your needs in the moment, and leaving the self-critic behind. A little bit of discipline can help us do what we want in life, but too much can lead to mental resistance, preventing you from practicing at all.

It is important to start with some conscious breathing in a comfortable seated position (on the floor or in a chair). Rather than forcing your breath in any way, allow it to flow naturally and just notice it. Bring your focus to your breath, and each time you find your mind wandering somewhere else, simply allow yourself to re-focus on your breath. Feel what it feels like to be in your own body and be your own self in this moment. This sets the stage for your practice to be real, true, and conscious.

After a few minutes of breathing, here are some suggestions for variations of your posture practice:

"Shake 'n breathe" warm-up

A simple, fantastic warm-up to do before practicing the yoga postures is a practice I call "shake 'n breathe." There are no rules. Start by bending and straightening your knees; this creates a little bouncing movement up and down. Breathe in and out every time you bob up and down. Next, shake your hands and wrists; as if you were flinging something off of your fingers. Let that movement travel up your arms and into your shoulders. From there, continue shaking, bouncing, shimmying, or wiggling every part of your body vigorously while breathing rhythmically.

Don't forget your head, hips, and spine. If you feel like jumping, let yourself jump. Start slowly and work up to a frenzied pace! Practice for at least 5 minutes and work up to 15 minutes or more. Let the movements take you over. Give it one hundred percent of your attention and energy. After you are into it fully, don't resist any type of movement that comes (unless you know it is not good for your health). You may even end up dancing. This warm-up jump starts your yoga practice. Not only does it get you warm, it is wonderful for releasing stress, and cultivating freedom and spontaneity of movement. Don't hold back.

Devalila Yoga freeze and flow

Use music with a light rhythm and follow the innate impulses of your body to move in and out of positions that you know, or invent in the moment. Release any concern about doing a pose correctly.

Sometimes you may feel like staying in a posture for a longer time, and sometimes you may flow swiftly from pose to pose. Trust your inner guidance as you freeze and flow.

Set Sequence flow

You may decide to practice the same set sequence of poses repetitively; like the classic yoga sun salutations, or daily yoga at your wall sequence in this book. The beauty is that once you have learned or memorized a sequence, you don't have to think about what comes next.

Static postures

Sometimes you may not feel like moving from pose to pose and your body may guide you into holding a posture for several minutes. You may want to stay in a pose until your body sends you a new idea, or tells you to move on. You may find yourself drawn to this style of practice when you want to focus inwardly and calm yourself. Let your breath keep flowing even though your movements are more static.

Repetition and counter postures

You can repeat the same pose several times with short rest periods in between, or perform the same pose with increasing depth or energy each time you do it. After repeating a pose several times you can then perform a counter posture that moves your body in the opposite direction from the pose before it. For example, you can flow from camel pose into child pose, upward dog into downward dog, or plow into a forward fold, just to name a few.

Restorative Poses

You can put yourself into simple poses using props to support your body for 5-20 minutes or longer. See section 5 for ideas.

Ending the practice

Always allow yourself time to finish your yoga practice with a couple of minutes (or hours) of just laying flat on your back, or sitting quietly. Experience your body and the after-effects of your practice.

Sticking with your practice

In the yoga practice we strive to find a balance between doing too much and doing too little, and we embrace discomfort instead of avoiding it. It can be a challenge to practice yoga. In the posture practice, we put our bodies into these contorted-looking positions and we attempt to keep breathing deeply and embracing our experience. What makes the yoga practice interesting, challenging, and different from regular exercise is its underlying intention to increase our awareness of everything: our bodies, spirit, thoughts, emotions, and our breath.

In yoga practice we aim to accept what is, breathe into it, and become present to what we are experiencing—pleasant or unpleasant. Ultimately, what we learn on our yoga mats we can apply to situations we encounter in our daily lives. This is easier said than done. Remember that it is a practice. Yoga is an ongoing process of unfolding, undoing, and unraveling layers of stress, misconceptions, patterns, and blocks to our true nature.

New students beginning to practice yoga postures may complain about the high level of sensations they experience, and can get easily discouraged. If they aren't accustomed to feeling strong sensations, they may be put off by the initial intensity of their feelings and give up too soon. If we are honest with ourselves and reflect on our past, we might admit that the most challenging times in our life gave us the most strength, and ultimately the most benefit. Isn't it true?

Stay with your yoga practice. It is a life-long relationship. Don't judge it too quickly.

Passages to recall while you are practicing

Relating to your body during practice...

- All postures have their value. What and when you practice, and how you practice depends on the time, the situation, the intent, your preference, and your physical, emotional and mental state at the moment.

- Soften your inner body and attitude. Repose in each pose.

- Get more playful and release competitiveness.

- Articulate the pose so that it falls somewhere between too hard and too easy.

- Reflect on how you could be more kind to yourself during your practice.

- Feel the flow and direction of energy in the poses.

- At any moment your breath is a reflection of your state of being. Become aware of it and use it as a tool for self reflection.

- Your body should be warmed up before doing most yoga postures.

- Pay attention to the small transitional movements between postures. Make them conscious and part of your practice.

- Even falling out of a balance posture is part of the practice. You can make falling a part of your practice. Fall with grace!

- Slow, methodical movements with keen awareness invite grace and peace into your life.

- Use micro movements to explore places in your body that you may not have noticed before.

- Give yourself time to feel and experience the sensations that are present when you release a pose after holding it for a time.

Relating to your breath during your practice...

- Pay attention to the movements your body makes when you breathe in and breathe out.

- Yoga posture practice is a moving meditation. Your breath and body sensations are the focus of the meditation.

- Feel how your spine naturally undulates as you breathe.

- Notice the wave-like movement of your breath in your abdominal area and chest.

- Notice how your body lengthens and expands on the inhale.

- Notice how your body relaxes and contracts on the exhale.

- Attempt to breathe into your back lungs and ribs, not just in the front.

- Attempt to expand your breath laterally into your sides and side ribs.

- Listen for the sound of your breath as you practice. The sound should come more from the back of your throat than from your nostrils or mouth.

- When your mind wanders bring it back to your breath.

- Notice the natural rhythm or pulsation of your breath going from activity to stillness.

- When you move deeper into a folding or twisting posture, move on the exhalation.

- When you move deeper into a lifting, reaching, expanding or arching posture, move on the inhalation.

- When you feel an area of tension or strong sensation in your body, direct your breath toward or into that area.

- Use your breath to inform you. When you have lost your focus, your breath may become shallow and shaky. If you are exerting too much energy your breath may become rushed or uneven.

Relating to your mind during your practice...

- The yoga postures are a metaphor for the challenging life situations we encounter. When we practice breathing into strong, uncomfortable sensations, we are actually preparing ourselves for whatever difficulties may arise in life itself.

- What you are thinking in a yoga posture may have much more effect on your body than what you are physically doing in the posture. Thinking fearful thoughts can actually create more tension when you are attempting to relax and lengthen. Be aware of your mental tendencies. Question their validity, and challenge their truthfulness.

- You cannot fail or be "horrible" at yoga so it is better to let this thought go as soon as possible.

- Having a more flexible hamstring muscle will not necessarily make you a more centered, loving, and peaceful human being. Drop the idea that yoga is just about flexibility!

- Notice what you are thinking when you become aware that you are holding your breath. Is there any correlation to your level of stress and tension?

- Don't worry so much about getting the posture "perfect."

- As for your mind: don't fight your thoughts, but don't believe them either, unless of course you feel like it!

Relating to your emotions during practice...

- Practice makes the heart grow fonder.

- You don't always have to do the same thing when you practice. If you don't feel like doing yoga postures today; simply sit and breathe. What would emotionally uplift you today?

- Be natural. If emotions come, let them come.

- You are very likely to encounter yourself during the practice! There is nothing to fear. You are the one you live with.

- Close your eyes and feel what you feel.

- Focus on inner experiences during your practice.

- Discomfort is an excellent object for the focus of your meditation. It naturally and organically attracts your attention.

- Each tension or emotion that you experience during your yoga practice provides a means for you to focus more deeply.

- Explore places in your body that feel tense, blocked, tight, stiff, or painful.

Gentle reminders to take the pressure off of yourself...

- Just as a seedling contains the potential for a whole tree to exist, the beginning stages of practicing a pose, however tiny, contain the full complete pose.

- Don't be afraid of making a fool of yourself while you're practicing. It's normal for the yoga postures to be awkward at first. Don't take the practice too seriously. You will not be graded.

- Explore what is happening right now. It is all you have to work with.

- The past is gone and the future is going.

Yoga props to support your practice

Yoga props such as sticky mats, blocks, pillows, blankets, and straps allow you to modify a pose to your body type and skill level, and add an extra level of safety to your practice. Take a look at the photos below to get an idea of how to use the props:

Using a yoga mat

Yoga mats with non-skid surfaces increase your level of safety during your practice. The slightly tacky surface keeps your mat from sliding on the floor, and also helps you to stabilize your contact with the floor in the foundation of the yoga posture.

Line up the short edge of your yoga sticky mat with the edge of the wall for certain poses that extend away from the wall.

Line up the long edge of your yoga sticky mat with the edge of the wall for certain poses that require a fuller body contact with the wall.

Using yoga blocks

Yoga blocks bridge the distance between you and the floor, or you and the wall. They help you balance when you can't reach the floor. Blocks help you safely go deeper into a pose, and can be used to support you when you feel too much sensation in the posture. Make sure the blocks are stable before you press into them. Here are a few examples:

Place blocks under your hands and against a wall in wheel pose.

Place a block between your knee and the wall in warrior 1 pose.

Place blocks under your hands in a standing pose like pyramid.

Place blocks under your hands in a runner's lunge pose.

Using a strap or tie

A yoga tie or strap can bridge the distance between your two hands, or between your hand and your foot. You can also place a strap around your arms or legs to hold them in place during certain yoga poses. Here are a few examples:

Hold a strap between your hands in yoga Mudra pose to bridge the distance between hands if your shoulders are tight and you cannot comfortably clasp your hands.

Place a strap around your upper arms to hold them steady and properly aligned during poses like low plank, high plank, dolphin, and peacock feather.

Using a blanket

There are many ways to use a blanket to support you and provide safety and comfort during your yoga practice. Here are examples:

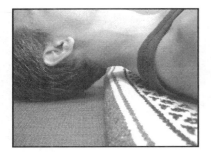

Fold the blanket into a rectangular or square shape and place it under your shoulders for support in poses like shoulder stand, bridge, and plow. Using a blanket in this way prevents your cervical spine from crunching into the floor.

Roll the blanket into a bolster shape and place it under your knees in forward folding type poses.

Lay the blanket flat under your head for comfort in restorative poses.

Roll a blanket into a bolster shape, tie a strap around it to keep the form, and place it between your head and the wall during handstand pose.

Making contact with the wall

To get the most benefit out of your yoga at the wall practice, it is important to know how to interact and align yourself with the wall. The parts of your body that make direct contact with the wall are the areas where you will lean, press, and push into the wall.

Some examples of body contact with the wall:

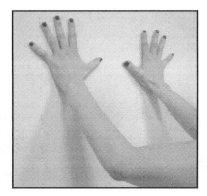

In postures like wall press, or at other times when hand contact is required, your hands should make full contact with the wall. To help anchor your hand, press firmly down on the knuckle of your index finger and spread your fingers as much as possible. Your index finger should point vertically or slightly to the outside.

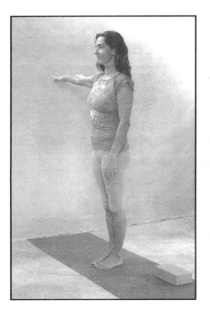

There are poses such as forward leg extension, warrior 3, and half moon 2 where you must gauge your leg distance from the wall so that your leg has space to fully extend. You can get a good approximation of your extended leg length by stretching your arm out to the side, touching your fingertips to the wall. After you make the measurement, turn around and bring your leg up into the posture.

There are a few cases where you can lightly touch your head to the wall to help with alignment and support. Move slowly as your head approaches the wall, and be extra conscious of the space between you and the wall.

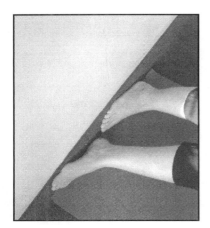

In postures like side plank, or when required, attempt to keep your feet flat against the wall just as if you were walking on the wall. Press your heel and the joints under your pinky toe/ball of your foot into the wall. Avoid curling or gripping your toes.

For postures like the forearm wall press which call for placing your forearms on the wall, attempt to keep your forearms parallel to one another. Avoid laterally bending your wrists. Press firmly into the wall and stay away from letting your elbows slide out away from each other.

Keep your elbows straightened and your shoulders moving downward away from your ears for postures such as the wall press where you are required to press your hands into the wall.

In the case of postures such as dangling forward fold where you press your sit bones against the wall, your heels should not be touching the wall. Your heels can be as little as a few inches away from the wall, or as much as a foot. Experiment with your foot placement. I strongly suggest that you **bend your knees in any of the forward folding postures.** By bending your knees you relax the hamstring muscles and lessen the strain on your lower back.

In some postures, such as tree pose, you can lightly touch your knee to the wall to aid with balance and stability. Be sure to allow enough space between your body and the wall so that your hip expresses its full range of motion.

Postures such as pigeon preparation pose or other deep quadricep stretches require you to press your shin against the wall with your knee on the floor. Start on all fours and very carefully slide your knee back as you bring your shin up to the wall. Be gentle with your knees, and it is a good idea to place a blanket flat beneath your knee cap.

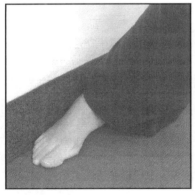

In standing poses such as warrior 2, keep your foot flat on the floor when you press the outside edge of your foot into the wall. Avoid over-lifting the arch of your foot.

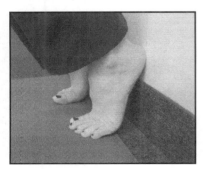

In poses such as runner's lunge, downward dog, and dolphin you can put your heels up on the wall as an optional foot variation that increases the stretch in the back of your legs. When the heels are on the wall, the balls of your feet and your toes should stay on the floor.

Yoga Postures at Your Wall
for Strength and Energy

Focus on Strength and Energy

These poses cultivate strength in our bodies, and the benefits are not limited to strengthening. Any yoga posture has the potential to develop greater strength, energy, flexibility, **and** relaxation in us. Your perception of the benefits may shift daily and over the years.

Visit this section of the book when you want to become physically stronger, release stress, or need a mental or physical boost of energy. You may find yourself drawn to this section when you have been sitting for long periods of time, or when you yearn for an increase in your physical energy and warmth.

Postures that focus on strength build feelings of confidence, stability, success, and purpose. The only way you will know how these poses benefit you is to experiment with them and observe the results. Consider all of the poses as you explore the infinite options for creating a yoga practice that suits you.

As you practice these poses, keep these words in mind: fortify, boost, engage, uplift, energize, build, charge, warm, harness, reinforce, and refresh.

Specific tips for practicing the postures in this section:

- Perform each posture for at least 30 seconds or longer. The duration depends on your mood, experience level, and your needs.

- Warm-up before starting the wall practice for strength. Jog in place, jump up and down, ride your bike, do a few jumping jacks, practice the "brushing the floor" warm-up described in this section, or practice the "shake 'n' breathe" technique described in the first section.

- Standing poses may be physically challenging for you. At first, you may not be able to hold these postures for very long. Performing yoga postures at the wall may add an additional degree of challenge to the same poses you practice free-standing on your mat. Little by little, you may increase your time in a posture.

• Listen to your body. Some days you have more energy and are able to hold the postures longer. Other days you may need to take it a little easier. Create your practice moment by moment in the present moment—this expresses the true flexibility of yoga.

• Read the precautions and be aware of your limitations. Be extremely sensible and careful when you attempt the handstand and headstand poses.

"Brush The Floor" Warm-up

Level of difficulty: Beginner

Focus and Intention: Warming up, letting go of stress, spinal flexion & extension, activating your legs

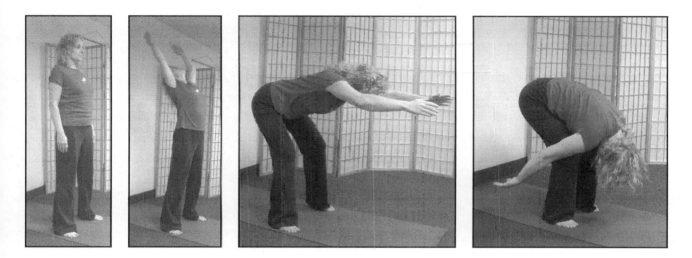

Instructions at a glance

- Stand with your feet wider than hip width apart, a giant step **away** from objects and the wall (Figure 1). Your toes are pointed forward.

- Relax your arms at your sides.

- Inhale deeply as you sweep your arms over your head, arching backwards slightly.

- Sweep your arms to the floor and exhale through your mouth with a "ha!" sound.

- Bend your knees so that your fingertips gently brush the floor beside your feet.

- Relax your head and neck when folding over your legs.

- Look to the ceiling when you arch, and look to your knees when you bend over.

- Continue this movement for a few minutes, gradually gaining speed and momentum.

- As a variation, position your feet farther apart and sweep your hands between them rather than beside them.

Precautions

- If you feel dizzy or unstable, slow the movement down and/or widen your stance.

- Use caution if you have high or low blood pressure.

Mountain Pose At The Wall

Level of difficulty:	Beginner
Focus and Intention:	Postural alignment, centering, steadiness

  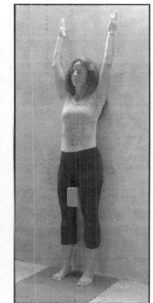

Instructions at a glance

- Back up to the wall until your buttocks touch.

- Stand with your heels a few inches from the wall..

- Coax your shoulder blades, triceps, and the back of your head toward the wall.

- Drop your shoulders away from your ears.

- Focus your eyes on a point eye level in front of you.

- Follow the suggestions below for experimenting with this posture.

Mountain Pose Variation—"cactus" arms with block

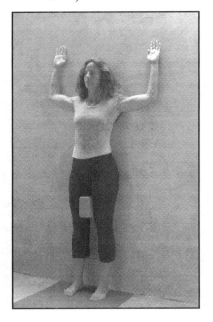

Instructions at a glance

- Bring your arms up to shoulder height and attempt to keep them at this height.

- Bend your elbows at a ninety degree angle.

- Press your shoulders and arms into the wall.

- Drop your shoulders away from your ears.

- Spread your fingers and press the backs of your hands and wrists toward the wall.

- Focus your eyes on a point eye level in front of you.

Tips for getting into the pose

1. Don't force your lower back or neck to the wall.

2. Allow the natural curves of your spine to just be there.

Exiting the pose

Slightly bend your knees and take a step forward, moving away from the wall.

Yoga prop suggestions

Squeeze a yoga block between your knees or inner thighs to align and stimulate your legs.

Ideas for breathing in the pose

On your inhalations, intentionally expand your breath into your side and back ribs. On your exhalations, feel the outer surfaces of your body drawing inward toward the inner core of your body as if you were tying a corset around your abdomen.

Suggestion for visual focus

Let your eyes focus on a point about eye level in front of you. You can also close your eyes and feel your physical body, the solidity of the wall, and the space around your body.

Imagery for alignment

Grow taller with each inhalation.

Imagine balancing a bowl on the top of your head. Graciously offer its contents to the sky above you.

When you exhale, visualize roots extending from your navel down through your legs and through the soles of your feet into the center of the Earth.

"Home Play" experiments—exploring and deepening the posture

Take at least 30 seconds to feel each part of your body or the area around you. Notice every detail about yourself; standing tall with your friend, the wall.

Lift your toes up and press into the balls of your feet, then relax your toes back to the floor.

Shift your weight slowly from the left to the right, forward and then back. Slightly bend your knees, and connect to the ground beneath you.

Try firming up your legs, flexing your quadriceps (your thigh muscles) to feel the strength, support and stability of your lower body. Feel your muscles hugging your leg bones.

Tinker with tilting your pelvis a little forward and then backward, to find a position that feels balanced to you.

Roll your shoulders up toward your ears, and then down and slightly back until you feel a slight expansion in your chest. Experiment with the position of your head and neck in relation to your shoulders.

When you finish exploring your body and sensations, feel the space in front of you, to the sides, and in back of you.

Possible benefits and experiences of the pose

- Promotes stability and centeredness.

- Increases your awareness of your posture.

- Improves postural alignment.

- Strengthens the legs and lower body.

- Strengthens the upper back.

Chair Pose At The Wall

Level of difficulty: Beginner

Focus and Intention: Leg strength, stability, stamina, endurance

Instructions at a glance

- Separate your feet a few inches apart with your toes pointing straight ahead.

- For a more challenging standing position, bring your feet closer together.

- Stand closer to your wall to perform chair pose with an average bend in your knees – about 5 to 7 inches.

- Stand further from your wall to perform chair pose with a greater bend in your knees.

- Bend your knees until your buttocks touch the wall.

- Sit against the wall as if you were sitting onto a chair behind you.

• Aim your knees straight ahead; not pointing inward or outward.

• Pull your navel toward your lower back.

• Tuck your hips to achieve a neutral pelvic position.

• Bring your front ribs inward.

• Raise your arms to shoulder height in front of you, palms down (Figure 1).

• Drop your shoulders away from your ears.

• Soften your facial muscles and jaw line and unclench your teeth!

• To challenge your upper body, extend your arms over your head with your palms facing each other (Figure 2).

Tips for getting into the pose

1. Your distance from the wall greatly affects the physical demand on your legs. The further you are from the wall, the more you have to bend your knees to make contact. A shorter distance challenges your legs less, and therefore requires less effort.

2. If your shoulders hunch, elongate your spine to avoid leaning forward.

3. When reaching your arms overhead, sweep them out to the side in a large circular motion, and then up over your head.

4. Align your knees directly over your toes so as not to see the inner or outer edges of your feet when you look down.

5. Avoid curling your toes or gripping the floor with them.

6. Relax your jaw.

7. Unclench your teeth.

Exiting the pose

Lower your arms. Straighten your legs and step away from the wall.

Yoga prop suggestions

Squeeze a yoga block between your knees or inner thighs to align and activate your legs.

Squeeze a yoga block between your hands to strengthen your arms.

Suggestions for breathing in the pose

When the pose becomes more intense, maintain an even, smooth breathing pattern. On your incoming breaths, feel the expansion and movement of your breath into your side and back ribs. On your outgoing breaths, contract your diaphragm area to effectively squeeze the carbon dioxide from your lungs.

Suggestion for visual focus

Look at a point eye level in front of you. If you are feeling over heated or off balance, look at a point on the floor in front of you.

Imagery for alignment

My favorite imagery for alignment in this pose is squatting over a toilet seat in a bus station bathroom. My students suggest I try for something more positive. So…

To get into chair pose, imagine you are standing at the edge of a refreshing swimming pool getting ready to dive into the pool. Instinctively, you bend your knees and swing your arms to gain momentum for your dive.

In chair pose, please don't dive off the edge. Remain in the "dive ready" position with the spirit of anticipation and determination.

"Home Play" experiments—exploring and deepening the posture

Tilt your pelvis a little forward, then a little backward until you find a position that feels neutral.

Increase the bend in your knees, but do not let your hips drop below your knee level, to experiment with the depth of the pose.

Vary your torso position between being upright, and then inclined, and notice the changes in your experience of the posture.

Spread your toes to achieve an even distribution of your weight in your feet.

Slowly increase the time you stay in this pose. Discover how you can remain centered if/when the posture becomes more demanding.

Become aware of what you are thinking at that time. Label it "thinking," and bring your attention back to your breath.

Notice if your tendency is to push yourself, or to back away. Consciously relax the parts of your body that do not require exertion.

Possible benefits and experiences of the pose

- Promotes stability and a feeling of being grounded.

- Strengthens the legs, especially the quadriceps.

- Develops endurance and determination.

- An excellent warm up for downhill skiing.

Precautions

- Prevent knee strain by pointing your knees forward, and not over-bending them.

- Prevent discomfort in your lower back by not arching or rounding your lower back, always seek a neutral position.

Chair pose variation—"cactus" arms

Instructions at a glance

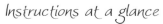

- From chair pose, lean your back against the wall.

- Raise your arms to shoulder height and maintain them at this height.

- Bend your elbows at a ninety degree angle.

- Press your shoulders and arms into the wall.

- Relax your shoulders and press them down from your ears.

- Spread your fingers, pressing the backs of your hands and wrists against the wall.

- Enjoy the extra strengthening in your arms and legs!

- To exit the pose, lean away from the wall and straighten your legs.

Crossed Leg Chair Pose At The Wall

Level of difficulty: Beginner/Intermediate

Focus and Intention: Leg strength, hip flexibility, balance

Instructions at a glance

- Stand about a foot from the wall with your feet together and two yoga blocks placed in front of you as shown above (Figure 1).

- Stand about 5 to 7 inches from your wall for an easier variation.

- Bend your knees until your buttocks are touching the wall.

- Sit toward the wall as if you were sitting onto a chair behind you.

- Cross your ankle just above your other knee (Figure 2).

- Press your navel toward your lower back, tucking your hips, to achieve a neutral pelvic position.

- Lean your torso forward bringing your chest as close to your thighs as possible.

- Place your fingertips on yoga blocks for support (Figure 3).

- Wrap your arms around your bent leg as if you were cradling a baby (Figure 4).

- Press your shoulders away from your ears and elongate your spine.

- To deepen the pose, lower your body closer to the floor.

- Repeat the pose on the other leg (Figure 5).

Tips for getting into the pose

1. Your distance from the wall greatly affects the physical demand on your legs. The further you are from the wall, the more you have to bend your knees to make contact. A shorter distance places fewer demands on your legs, and therefore requires less effort.

2. If you feel too much discomfort in your bent knee and hip, straighten up more.

Exiting the pose

Unclasp your leg, uncross it, lift your bent knee toward your chest, and then place your foot on the floor. Stand upright.

Yoga prop suggestions

Place two yoga blocks on the floor in front of you for support when you bend into the pose.

Suggestions for breathing in the pose

Breathe into your hips. Of course, there are no lungs there, but the muscles of your hips and abdomen are connected to your diaphragm muscle and will be affected by your breath. Notice the movement of your breath in your hips.

Suggestion for visual focus

Look at a point on the floor in front of you.

Imagery for alignment

Imagine you are sitting with your leg crossed in a small chair designed for an infant. It is the only chair your host has, and you don't want to appear to be uncomfortable. Breathe and relax into the tiny chair. Your crossed leg opens in a very informal position. When you rise from the chair, do so slowly so you don't knock it over!

"Home Play" experiments—exploring and deepening the posture

Tilt your pelvis a little forward, then a little backward until you find a position that brings the greatest sensation in opening your hip.

Increase the bend in your knees and hug your leg more to experiment with the depth of the pose.

Vary your torso position between being upright, and then inclined. Notice the changes in your experience of the posture.

Disengage from this pose very slowly and carefully. Increase your awareness of your leg sensations when you release the pose.

Possible benefits and experiences of the pose

- Promotes flexibility in the hips and knees.

- Strengthens the legs, especially the quadriceps.

- Develops patience and forbearance.

Precautions

- Prevent knee strain by crossing and uncrossing your knees slowly.

- Prevent ankle strain by flexing the foot of your bent knee.

- Avoid bending or twisting your ankle.

Warrior 1 Pose At The Wall

Level of difficulty: Beginner

Focus and Intention: Leg strength, determination, perseverance

Instructions at a glance

- Stand with your back to the wall.

- Take a giant step forward with one foot.

- Or, stand about one leg's length in front of the wall and take a giant step backward.

- Bend your front knee and align it over your ankle, or slightly behind it. Adjust your leg position accordingly.

- Press the heel of your back foot firmly into the wall. Your toes remain on the floor.

- Straighten and activate your back leg as you keep your hip bones facing forward.

- Extend your arms overhead with palms facing each other. Bring life to your arms— you are a warrior/warrioress (Figure 2).

• Maintain a relaxed facial position—soften your face and jaw—smile!

• Perform the pose on the other leg (Figure 2).

Tips for getting into the pose

1. Experiment with the two different approaches to this pose mentioned above to discover which one feels more comfortable.

2. Energetically press your back heel into the wall and straighten your back knee as much as possible.

3. Separate your legs farther apart if you desire more physical challenge in the pose.

4. When raising your arms overhead, begin this movement by sweeping your arms backward and then over your head—as if you were opening your wings to fly. This movement encourages maximum range of motion and comfort in your shoulder area.

5. Poses such as downward dog and the runner's lunge are good transitional poses for entering warrior 1 pose.

Exiting the pose

Bring your hands down to the floor beside your front foot (lunge position). Lean your body forward and step your back leg forward. Stand upright.

Yoga prop suggestions

Squeeze a yoga block between your hands to energize and awaken your arms.

Suggestions for breathing in the pose

Breathe deeply into your upper chest. Notice a slight elevation of your upper body with your inhalations—as if you were growing taller. Feel your outgoing breath converging around your diaphragm and navel.

Section 2: Yoga Postures at Your Wall for Strength and Energy

Suggestion for visual focus

Focus on a point eye level in front of you. If you are feeling overheated, or off balance, look to a point on the floor.

Imagery for alignment

Imagine that you are attempting to split your yoga mat in half with the strength of your legs. Feel your legs moving in opposite directions.

Be in this pose as you imagine a warrior would. Imagine you are wearing a protective shield across your chest. Your arms are strong, your heart filled with courage, as you prepare for battle.

"Home Play" experiments—exploring and deepening the pose

During warrior 1 pose summon feelings of courage and determination.

When you face real or perceived obstacles in your life, practice this pose during your yoga at the wall session. Breathe deeply with the knowledge and confidence that you will act according to the best interests of everyone involved.

Shift your awareness between your back leg and your front leg.

Feel the opposite forces of energy in your body in this pose: energy rising upward through your arms, and also downward through your legs.

Experiment with bending your front leg more, and then less. Keep your back heel anchored to the wall. Notice the changes in sensations in your leg muscles.

Lift your ribs away from your hips without jutting them forward.

Notice your facial expression. Strive to loosen your jaw and relax your forehead.

Possible benefits and experiences of the pose

- Cultivates a sense of presence and connection.

- Strengthens the legs and lower body.

- Develops a sense of courage, confidence, and inner strength.

Precautions

- For the safety of your knees, do not allow your bent knee to move in front of your ankle. Align it **over** your ankle.

- Use caution when easing your heel back into the wall.

Warrior 1 pose variation—back foot down

Instructions at a glance

- From the raised heel foot position, lower your heel to the floor maintaining contact with the wall.

- Turn your back foot to face forward at a 45 degree angle to the wall (about the size of an average pizza slice).

- Press the outer edge of your heel into the wall as you perform the pose.

- Press your shoulders away from your ears.

- To exit the pose, step your back leg forward and perform the pose on the other leg.

- This variation offers more lateral hip rotation in the back leg.

Warrior 1 pose variation—knee to block into the wall

Instructions at a glance

- Stand facing the wall about the distance of your yoga block.

- Place the yoga block in a horizontal position between your knee and the wall. Make sure it is stable before going further.

- Bend the knee and press it into the block (Figures 1 & 2).

- Extend your back leg into a long stance in one of the previously mentioned foot positions.

- Place your hands on your hips, or extend them over your head.

- Simultaneously press your knee toward the wall and your back foot toward the floor.

- To exit the pose, step your back foot forward, remove the block, and perform the pose on the other leg.

- This variation keeps your front knee aligned.

Warrior 2 Pose At The Wall

Level of difficulty: Beginner

Focus and Intention: Leg strength, stability, stamina, endurance

 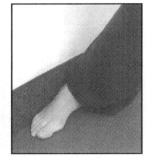

Instructions at a glance

- Stand about one leg's length or more in front of the wall.

- Take a giant step backward, pressing the outside edge of one foot against the wall.

- Turn your other foot to point directly away from the wall.

- Bend your front knee and align it over your ankle.

- Adjust your leg position until your knee is properly aligned over the ankle.

- Energetically press your back foot into the wall and maintain full foot contact with the floor.

- Straighten your back knee, and firm the muscles in your back leg.

- Extend your arms over your legs at shoulder height. Your back hand is pressing the wall.

- Press your shoulders down and expand your chest.

- Keep your torso aligned over your hips.

- Anchor your legs as you reach out through your hands.

- Create smooth, even lines of energy extending out from the mid line of your body to your outer extremities.

- Turn around and perform the pose on the other leg.

Tips for getting into the pose

1. Energetically press your back foot into the wall and straighten your back knee as much as possible.

2. Avoid thrusting your rib cage forward or over-arching your lower back.

3. Your arms, and even your fingers, participate in this pose.

4. Poses such as downward dog and the runner's lunge are good transitional poses for entering warrior 2 pose.

Exiting the pose

Relax your arms to your sides, turn your front foot forward, and step your feet together. Or, step the back foot forward to join the front foot.

Yoga prop suggestions

Press into the wall with your back foot and hand.

Suggestions for breathing in the pose

Breathe deeply into your upper chest and feel the breath extending into your fingertips. As you exhale, sink toward the floor and press your feet into the yoga mat.

Suggestion for visual focus

Focus on the middle finger of your front hand.

Imagery for alignment

Imagine your muscles are tight gloves or support hose wrapping and hugging your bones. Feel the energy, warmth, and strength of every muscle of your body as you practice warrior 2 pose.

"Home Play" experiments—exploring and deepening the pose

During warrior 2 pose, remember you have the power and so it's appropriate to summon feelings of tolerance and willpower.

Reflect on your purpose here on Earth. Whatever form your life takes at this moment; apply the steadfastness and resolve of a warrior.

Shift your awareness between your back leg and your front leg.

Feel the opposite forces of energy in your body in this pose: energy rising upward through your arms, and also downward through your legs.

Experiment with bending your front leg more, and then less, but do not extend your knee beyond your ankle.

Keep your back foot anchored to the wall. Notice the changes in sensations in your leg muscles.

Lift your ribs away from your hips without jutting them forward.

Possible benefits and experiences of the pose

- Cultivates willpower and fortifies the spirit.

- Strengthens the legs and lower body.

- Strengths the arms and expands the chest.

- Develops a sense of tenacity, courage and presence.

Precautions

For the safety of your knees, do not lunge your bent knee in front of your ankle. Align it **over** your ankle. Bring your knee back to a centered position if it collapses inward.

Warrior 2 pose variation—back to the wall

Instructions at a glance

- Stand with your rear end touching the wall.

- Turn your foot so that it is parallel to the wall, and about 3-4 inches away from it.

- Slide your back foot about one leg length or more away from your front foot.

- Press your back heel against the wall.

- Bend your front knee over the ankle.

- Stretch your arms at shoulder height.

- Look toward the middle finger of your front hand.

• Press your buttocks, shoulders, and arms into the wall.

• Repeat the pose on the other side.

• To exit the pose, turn away from the wall and step your feet together.

Downward Dog Pose At The Wall

Level of difficulty: Beginner/Intermediate

Focus and Intention: Back flexibility and strength, hip and leg flexibility, arm strength, circulation, mild inversion

 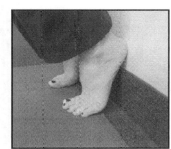

Instructions at a glance

> NOTE: Putting your heels up on the wall in downward dog encourages you to lift your hips and helps you extend your arms, shoulders, and lengthen your back.
>
> • Start on your hands and knees with the soles of your feet against the wall.
>
> • Place your hands shoulder width apart, and keep your arms straight (if you have elbows that hyperextend, keep them slightly bent).
>
> • Walk your hands about 5-7 inches forward until your wrists are no longer bent at a sharp angle.
>
> • Spread your fingers wide apart with your index fingers pointing straight ahead.
>
> • Straighten your legs and lift your hips in the air and toward the wall.
>
> • Reach your chest toward your knees.

- Look toward your navel.

- Push the balls of your feet into the floor and your heels into the wall.

- Press your shoulder blades away from your ears and toward your tail bone.

- Maintain a relaxed facial expression— soften your face and jaw line.

Tips for getting into the pose

1. If your shoulders hunch, press them down and rotate outward.

2. Lengthen your back like a telescope extending open.

3. Lengthen your neck by looking toward your navel.

Exiting the pose

Bend your knees and bring them to the floor, or walk your feet toward your hands and stand upright.

Yoga prop suggestions

Squeeze a yoga block between your knees or inner thighs to align and activate your legs.

Place your hands on yoga blocks to lessen the pressure on your wrists.

Suggestions for breathing in the poses

Inhale and fully lengthen your spine while expanding your chest. Exhale and let your abdomen become concave.

Suggestions for visual focus

Let your eyes focus on the area of your navel. If that feels too challenging, look at your knees.

Imagery for alignment

After observing dogs (and cats) performing this movement frequently, some wise yogi named this pose. I have noticed that my cats almost always do this pose after they eat. If you have a pet or have a chance to observe a dog or a cat, pay close attention to their downward dog stretches. Imagine your favorite dog or cat, or think of one you know; they perform this pose as casually as they do everything else in their moment-to-moment lives. Let yourself move as freely and playfully as they do without judgment or self-consciousness. For them there is no "perfect" pose, nor thoughts about the flexibility of their legs. They move, breathe, and stretch for the pure joy of it. Allow yourself to do the same. What the heck, go for it-give a howl, growl, bark, hiss, or meow if you feel like it!

"Home Play" experiments—exploring and deepening the pose

Explore the 4 elements—earth, air, fire, and water—at play in your body as you hold this pose for an extended period of time.

First, feel the fire element in the heat and warmth of your muscles. Make the fire stronger by hugging your muscles to your bones. Notice your inner body temperature and the heat radiating from with you. Feel "firey." Feel hotness.

Next, feel the water element by letting your body explore freely in the pose. Sway your hips, move your feet, bend and straighten knees and elbows. Become aware of the water in your mouth, eyes, intestines, and bladder. Feel "watery." Feel coolness.

Then, feel the earth element manifesting in you as the hard and boney parts of your body. Feel your bones supporting you in downward dog pose. Feel the solidity and foundation of your bones in your body. Notice the hardness of your teeth. Feel "Earthy." You "ROCK!"

Lastly, feel the air element within your lungs and all around your body. Feel the flow of air entering and exiting your body in a harmonious exchange with your environment. Feel the contact of the air on your skin. Is it warm, cool? Feel the temperature of the air flowing into your nostrils. Focus on feeling buoyant as you let your hips float toward the ceiling. Feel "airy." Soar!

Possible benefits and experiences of the pose

- Promotes flexibility in the back of the body.

- Increases energy and circulation.

- Strengthens arms, shoulders, and legs.

- Develops endurance and steadiness.

Precautions

- Downward dog is considered a mild inversion because your head drops below your heart. If you have high blood pressure, you may want to limit your time in this pose and work into it slowly and gradually. Consult your doctor if you have doubts or questions.

- If you feel discomfort in your wrist and shoulder joints, limit your time in this pose at the beginning.

- Perform the standing wall press pose instead if you have concerns about practicing inverted poses.

Downward dog pose easier variation—bent knees

Instructions at a glance

- Follow the instructions for the main pose except bend your knees.

- Keep reaching your chest toward your thighs and lengthen your back.

Downward dog pose variation—heels down

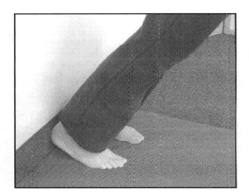

Instructions at a glance

• From the downward dog heels up on the wall position, place your feet on the floor.

• Adjust your foot position for your heels to press firmly into the wall. The bottoms of your feet may not completely contact the floor.

• Lift your pelvis/tail bone up in the air and toward the wall.

• Evenly distribute your weight on your hands.

• Reach your chest toward your knees.

• To exit the pose, bend your knees and bring them to the floor, or walk your feet toward your hands and stand upright.

• This variation provides a little extra stretch in the backs of your legs.

Downward dog pose variation—one leg in the air

Instructions at a glance

• From the downward dog heels up on the wall position, extend one of your legs up toward the wall.

• Press the top of your raised foot into the wall and point your toes.

• Press your pelvis toward the wall and keep your hips squared.

• Evenly distribute your weight on your hands. Keep your arms strong and active.

• Reach your chest toward your knee.

• Return your foot to the floor and repeat the pose on the other leg.

Downward dog pose variation—wall split

Instructions at a glance

• From the one leg downward dog position, walk your hands toward the wall as you slide your leg up the wall.

• Press your pelvis and legs closer to the wall, as much as possible.

• Take your time and let your legs slowly release into this deep stretch.

• Keep your standing leg strong and firm.

• Move your torso/abdomen closer to your standing leg.

• Look toward the knee of your standing leg.

• Try to touch your nose to the knee of your standing leg.

• To exit the pose, walk your hands forward one at a time and place your foot back on the floor.

• Bend your knees and return to a kneeling position.

Dolphin Pose At The Wall

Level of difficulty: Beginner/Intermediate

Focus and Intention: Abdominal and back strength

Instructions at a glance

> NOTE: This pose (Figure 1) is similar to downward dog pose except that your forearms are on the floor.

- Start on your hands and knees with the balls of your feet and heels against the wall.

- Place your elbows on the floor beneath your shoulders and interlace your fingers.

- Straighten your legs and lift your hips in the air and toward the wall (Figure 1).

- Reach your chest toward your knees.

- Press forcefully into the floor with your forearms.

- Look toward your navel.

- Push the balls of your feet into the floor and your heels into the wall.

- Press your shoulder blades away from your ears and toward your tail bone.

• Stretch and elongate your spine.

• To do the "dolphin push-up," (Figure 2) exhale as you shift your body weight forward, reaching your chin toward your hands. Lower your hips toward the floor, but keep your abdomen strong.

• Lift your hips again (Figure 2).

• Alternate between the 2 positions 5-10 times—or more if you have the energy!

Tips for getting into the pose

1. If your shoulders hunch, press them down and rotate outward.

2. Keep your elbows in position, shoulder width apart.

3. Lengthen your back like a telescope extending open.

4. Lengthen your neck by looking toward your navel.

5. To maintain stability and prevent slippage, wear a short sleeved shirt or roll up your sleeves so you can maintain contact between your skin and the yoga mat.

Exiting the pose

Bend your knees and bring them to the floor. Straighten your arms. Stand upright.

Yoga prop suggestions

Squeeze a yoga block between your knees or inner thighs to align and activate your legs.

Suggestions for breathing in the poses

Inhale and fully lengthen your spine and expand your chest. Exhale and feel as if you are completely emptying out, or becoming hollow around your navel area.

Suggestions for visual focus

In the first position, focus on your knees or navel. While in the push-up position, lock to the floor in front of your hands.

Imagery for alignment

Named for the playful, undulating movements dolphins make when they swim, this pose can add some fun to your practice. Allow your body to flow from one movement to the next in a continuous, graceful flow. Coordinate your breath with the action in this dance of the dolphin.

"Home Play" experiments—exploring and deepening the pose

Start with a few push-ups. Gradually, day by day, increase your number of push-ups.

Pull your navel toward your spine when you are at the lowest point in your push-up.

How can you use your exhalation to give you more strength during this movement?

Possible benefits and experiences of the pose

- Promotes flexibility in your back.

- Increases energy and circulation.

- Strengthens arms, shoulders, and legs.

- Develops endurance and steadiness.

- Strengthens the abdominal muscles.

Precautions

- Because your head drops below your heart, Dolphin pose is considered a mild inversion. If you have high blood pressure, you may want to limit your time in this pose and work into it slowly and gradually. Consult your doctor if you have doubts or questions.

- If you feel discomfort in your elbows or shoulder joints, limit your time in this pose in the beginning.

• Perform the standing wall press pose instead if you have concerns about practicing inverted poses.

Dolpin pose variation—hands flat

Instructions at a glance

• Start on your hands and knees with the balls of your feet and heels against the wall.

• Place your elbows on the floor beneath your shoulders and spread your fingers wide apart.

• Straighten your legs and lift your hips in the air and toward the wall (Figure 1).

• Follow the same instructions for the main pose, but keep your forearms parallel to each other.

The Standing Wall Press

Level of difficulty: Beginner

Focus and Intention: Shoulder, arm, and back flexibility, arm and back strength

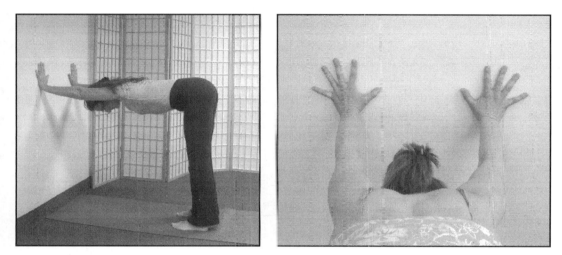

Instructions at a glance

- Stand about 2 feet or less from the wall and press your palms against the wall at about the height of your navel.

- Walk backwards as you let your chest, arms, and torso extend until you form an upside down letter "L" (Figure 1).

- Push into the wall as you push your hips in the other direction.

- Keep your arms parallel to each other and the floor. Press your shoulders down (Figure 2).

- Lengthen and strengthen your spine as you push.

- Don't sway your back like an old horse or cow. Your lower back is long as your ribs move toward your abdomen.

- Breathe deeply, allowing your chest and shoulders to relax more with each exhalation.

Tips for getting into the pose

1. Keep your legs slightly bent if you feel discomfort in your knees.

2. Spread your fingers as wide apart as possible.

3. Align your head and neck with your spine. Let your heart area melt towards the Earth.

4. Avoid scrunching your shoulders. Keep your shoulders down away from your ears.

Exiting the pose

Walk toward the wall and let your arms fall to your sides. Stand upright.

Yoga prop suggestions

Place a yoga block between your inner knees or upper thighs to activate your legs and maintain your leg alignment.

Suggestions for breathing in the pose

Inhale slowly as if you are trying to gradually fill your lungs up to your collar bone and between your shoulder blades.

Suggestion for visual focus

Let your eyes focus on a point on the wall. As you go deeper into the posture, look to a point on the floor beneath you.

Imagery for alignment

Visualize your body making the perfect capital letter "L" upside down. Construct a strong horizontal line with your back and lengthy vertical line with your legs. Explore words that begin with the letter "L" which can help you articulate this pose: long, languid, luxurious, loving, luminous, lengthened, longitude, latitude, leverage, loose, and lean.

"Home Play" experiments—exploring and deepening the posture

Lean your weight into your hands, but don't bend your elbows. Feel as if you could actually push the wall off of its foundation.

Bend your elbows a little and then straighten them again with more intention and strength.

Experiment with your hand and foot placement. Walk a few inches backward or forward. Raise or lower your hands a few inches. Find the position that allows you to express the most "L" words.

Possible benefits and experiences of the pose

- Promotes openness and expansion in the chest and shoulders.

- Stretches the muscles of the arms, upper back, and shoulder girdle.

- Cultivates greater range of motion in the shoulders.

- Releases shoulder tension and stress.

- For those who cannot invert their bodies, the wall push is a good substitute for downward dog and dolphin poses.

Precautions

- Keep your spine straight and strong to prevent over arching your lower back.

- Slightly bend your legs if you have a tendency to hyperextend in your knee joints.

Triangle Pose At The Wall

Level of difficulty: Beginner

Focus and Intention: Leg strength, stability, side stretch, chest expansion

Triangle pose variation—wider leg stance

Instructions at a glance

- If you are using a yoga block, place it next to the wall behind your front shin.

- Stand about 4-5 inches from the wall and spread your legs about one leg length apart (Figure 1), or wider (Figure 4).

- Turn your front foot forward, parallel to the wall.

- Press your back heel into the wall. Your buttocks may slightly contact the wall.

- Raise your arms to shoulder height and reach over your front foot, as your hips move in the other direction (Figure 1).

- Place your hand on your front thigh, shin, or on the yoga block —where ever you can reach without breaking contact with the wall.

- Put the hand of your upper arm behind your head and roll your upper body toward the wall (Figure 2).

- Straighten your legs by hugging your muscles toward your bones.

- Let the wall support you and help you keep your torso aligned with your front leg!

- Roll your torso open; leaning your shoulders, arms, and hips into the wall.

- Align your top arm with your lower arm (Figure 3).

- Send the energy from your core into your limbs.

- Turn your head and focus on a point on the ceiling, or toward the thumbnail of your upper hand.

- Let the wall support you.

- Keep your legs full of life.

- Breathe deeply and expand into your fingertips and feet.

- Repeat the pose on the other side of your body.

Tips for getting into the pose

1. If you have pain or discomfort in your front knee, bend it slightly.

2. Align your head and neck with your spine.

3. If you feel tightness in your lower back or hips, widen your stance.

Exiting the pose

Inhale and bring your arms and torso upright, relax your arms to your sides, and step your feet together.

Yoga prop suggestions

Place one or two yoga blocks under your front hand to lessen the distance between your arm and the floor.

Suggestions for breathing in the pose

If the pose becomes more challenging, maintain an even and smooth breathing pattern. On your exhalations, firm the region from your diaphragm to your navel. On your inhalations, feel the expansion and movement of your breath into your upper chest and upper back.

Suggestion for visual focus

First, focus on a point on the floor.

When you have established your balance, look to a point in the room or on the opposite wall. Then, look at your thumbnail (if your arm is in the air).

Imagery for alignment

How many triangles is your body making in this posture? Create strong angles and long lines with your body as you form these triangular shapes. Locate the 3 points of each triangle in your body position.

"Home Play" experiments—exploring and deepening the posture

Experiment with the placement of your lower hand. At first, place the hand on your thigh just above your knee. As you breathe, relax into the pose and move your hand to your shin, or to a yoga block. Your fingertips or hand may touch the floor to the outside of your front leg.

Try holding onto your big toe with your index and middle fingers, but do not lose contact with the wall.

Widen or narrow your leg stance, the base of your triangle, and feel the shifts in sensation in your legs and hips.

Allow the wall to challenge you: keep your torso upright, your chest and arms open wide, and your head in alignment with your body.

Possible benefits and experiences of the pose

- Promotes openness and expansion in the chest and shoulders.

- Strengthens the quadriceps and the legs.

- Cultivates balance and stability.

- Stretches the sides of the body.

Precautions

- Keep your front knee and big toe in alignment to prevent knee strain.

- Slightly bend your standing leg if you have a tendency to hyperextend your knee joints.

Extended Angle Pose At The Wall

Level of difficulty: Beginner/Intermediate

Focus and Intention: Leg strength and flexibility, shoulder flexibility, torso twist,
energizing, healing

Instructions at a glance

- If you are using a yoga block, place it to the inside of your front foot.

- Stand about 4-5 inches from the wall and spread your legs about one leg length apart or wider.

- Turn your front foot forward, parallel to the wall.

- Press your back heel into the wall. Your buttocks may slightly contact the wall.

- Bend your front knee until it aligns with your ankle.

- Raise your arms to shoulder height and reach over your front foot, as your hips move in the other direction.

- Place your forearm on your front thigh without breaking contact with the wall (Figure 1).

- Put the hand of your upper arm behind your head and roll your upper body toward the wall (Figure 1).

- Then, press your fingertips or hand to the yoga block or floor in front of your foot.

- Press into your feet and strengthen your legs.

- Lower your pelvis toward the ground.

- Extend your other arm in the air over your head, palm facing down (Figure 2).

- Let the wall support you and help you keep your torso aligned with your front leg!

- Roll your torso toward the wall.

- Lean your shoulders, arms, and hips into the wall.

- Send the energy from your core into your limbs.

- Turn your head and focus on a point in the middle of the palm of your upper hand.

- Breathe deeply and expand from your fingertips to your toes.

- Repeat the pose on the other side of your body.

Tips for getting into the pose

1. Anchor your back foot to the ground.

2. Rotate your upper armpit and rib cage toward the ceiling.

3. The wider your leg stance, the better.

4. If you feel tightness in your lower back or hips, increase the width of your stance.

Exiting the pose

Inhale and bring your arms and torso upright, relax your arms to your sides, and step your feet together.

Yoga prop suggestions

Place one or two yoga blocks under your front hand to lessen the distance between your arm and the floor.

Suggestions for breathing in the pose

On your inhalations, reach through your arms. On your exhalations, rotate your torso more.

Suggestion for visual focus

Once you have established your balance, look to a point in the room or on the opposite wall. Then, look at a point in the middle of your palm over your head (if your arm is in the air).

Imagery for alignment

This pose gets its name from the strong right angle made by your front knee and the intense sideways extension of your body. Visualize your body making a right angle. The more you articulate this angle, the more strength and opening you will generate in your legs and hips.

"Home Play" experiments—exploring and deepening the posture

Experiment with the placement of your lower hand. At first, place your forearm on your thigh just above your knee. As you breathe deeply, sink into your hips and widen your stance.

Then, place your hand onto a yoga block. Can you go deeper? If so, move the block away and place your fingertips or hand onto the floor to the inside of your front leg.

Allow the wall to challenge you to keep your torso upright, and your chest and arms open wide.

Feel the warmth, strength and energy in your legs.

Possible benefits and experiences of the pose

• Promotes openness and expansion in the chest and shoulders.

• Strengthens the quadriceps and the legs.

• Stretches the legs and hips.

• Cultivates endurance and stamina.

• Stretches the sides of the body.

Precautions

• Keep your front knee aligned over your ankle to prevent knee strain.

• Return to an easier variation if you feel dizzy or over-heated.

Revolving Triangle Pose At The Wall

Level of difficulty: Beginner/Intermediate

Focus and Intention: Balance, leg strength, back/shoulder flexibility, energizing

Instructions at a glance

- If you are using a yoga block, place it next to the wall to the outside of your front foot.

- Stand sideways, about 4-5 inches from the wall with the top of the closest leg touching the wall.

- Step your foot back to spread your legs about one leg length apart or less (Figure 1).

- Your front foot is parallel to the wall. Your back foot is turned out slightly, about 45 degrees to the wall.

- Square your hips.

- Raise the arm farthest from the wall over your head (Figure 2).

- Reach your top hand forward and down to your shin, to the floor, or to a yoga block placed near the wall (Figure 3).

- Reach your other arm overhead and hug the wall to your chest (Figure 3).

- Straighten your legs by hugging your bones with your muscles, and pressing into your back heel.

- Embrace the wall to rotate your chest and shoulders open!

- Twist your torso and spine.

- Align your top arm with your lower arm (Figure 3).

- Send the energy from your core into your limbs.

- Turn your head and focus on a point on the ceiling, or on the thumbnail of your upper hand.

- Deepen your twist and maintain the life in your legs

- Breathe deeply and expand from your fingertips to your toes.

- Repeat the pose on the other side of your body.

Tips for getting into the pose

1. If you have pain or discomfort in your front knee, bend it slightly.

2. Align your head and neck with your spine.

3. The more you squeeze your inner thighs and square your hips, the more you can turn your torso and spine.

4. If you have difficulty pressing your back foot to the floor, shorten your stance and square your hips more.

Exiting the pose

Inhale and bring your arms and torso upright, relax your arms to your sides, and step your feet together.

Yoga prop suggestions

Place one or two yoga blocks under your front hand to lessen the distance between your arm and the floor.

Suggestions for breathing in the pose

On your exhalations, twist deeper by firming the region from your diaphragm to your navel. On your inhalations, expand your chest and lungs toward the wall.

Suggestion for visual focus

First, focus on a point on the floor.

When you have established your balance, look to the ceiling or your thumbnail of the upper arm.

Imagery for alignment

How many triangles does your body make in this posture? Do the triangles feel different in this rotating pose versus regular triangle pose? Even though you are twisting, you can still create strong angles and long line with your body as you form these triangular shapes.

Locate the 3 new points of each triangle in your body position.

"Home Play" experiments—exploring and deepening the posture

There is a lot going on in this pose all at once: balancing, twisting, strengthening, and stretching. As you hold the pose, pick just one of these aspects and focus on it for several breaths. Then shift your attention to another aspect and place your emphasis there.

Widen or narrow your leg stance, the base of your revolved triangle pose, and feel the shifts in sensation in your legs and hips.

Use the wall as leverage to twist further and deeper.

Possible benefits and experiences of the pose

- Promotes openness and expansion in the chest and shoulders.

- Strengthens the quadriceps and the legs.

- Cultivates coordination and patience.

- Stretches the back and muscles around the spine.

- Massages internal organs.

Precautions

- Keep your front knee and big toe in alignment to prevent knee strain.

- Slightly bend your standing leg if you have a tendency to hyperextend your knee joints.

Boat Pose At The Wall

Level of difficulty: Beginner/Intermediate
Focus and Intention: Abdominal and back strength

Instructions at a glance

- Sit on the floor, or on a blanket facing the wall. Extend your legs in front of you so that your feet comfortably reach the wall.

- For less support from the wall, sit farther away from the wall.

- Place your feet on the wall at about eye level, with your knees slightly bent. Steady yourself by lightly touching the floor beside you (Figure 1).

- With the strength of your abdominal muscles, lean your torso back and reach toward your shins (Figure 2).

- Straighten your legs and expand your chest toward your feet.

- Lengthen your back as you reach through the top of your head.

- Exhale deeply and engage your diaphragm and abdomen.

Tips for getting into the pose

1. Try lifting only one leg at a time for an easier variation.

2. Lift your chest with enthusiasm.

3. Avoid rounding your shoulders.

Exiting the pose

Bend your legs, place your hands on the floor, and return to a seated position.

Yoga prop suggestions

Place a flat blanket under your hips for comfort.

Squeeze a yoga block between your ankles or knees to energize your legs.

Suggestions for breathing in the pose

On your inhalation fill your upper lungs and back. On your exhalation, draw your navel toward your spine.

Suggestion for visual focus

Look at your toes. This action keeps your chest lifted.

Imagery for alignment

Imagine your body is creating the letter "V." Reach actively through your feet and head, the tops of the "V," and lengthen your lower back to create a sharper angle at the base.

"Home Play" experiments—exploring and deepening the pose

Slowly increase the time you stay in this pose. Discover how you can remain relaxed when the posture becomes more demanding.

What movements or style of breathing maintain your abdomen strength?

Each time you practice boat pose, vary your distance from the wall. Eventually practice with only the tips of your toes touching the wall, or remove your feet from the wall completely and balance on your own.

Possible benefits and experiences of the pose

Strengthens abdominal muscles and deep hip flexors.

Precautions

• Stay aware of your spine and pelvic alignment to prevent discomfort in your lower back.

• If you feel pain in your lower back, release the pose as soon as possible.

Boat pose variation—clothespin body

Instructions at a glance

• Sit about a foot from the wall on a blanket or yoga mat.

• Place your hands behind you for support as you extend your legs up the wall.

• Straighten your legs and hug your calves.

• Lean your torso toward one of your legs and pull it close to your chest with your hand (Figure 1).

• Put it back on the wall and bring the other leg close.

• Repeat this movement several times on each leg.

• Then, hug your legs and bring your whole torso close (Figure 2).

- Lengthen your back as you reach through the top of your head.

- Exhale deeply and engage your diaphragm and abdomen.

- Reach your chin toward your shins.

- Lift your chest with enthusiasm.

- Avoid rounding your shoulders.

- To exit the pose, bend your legs, place your hands on the floor, and return to a seated position.

Boat pose variation—wide legs holding big toes

Instructions at a glance

•Follow the instructions for boat pose and separate your legs into a wide "V" position.

- Press your **heels** into the wall.

- Grasp the inside of your big toes with your index and middle finger.

- With the strength of your abdominal muscles, lean your torso back and lengthen your arms

- Straighten your legs and expand your chest toward the wall.

- Lengthen your back as you reach through the top of your head.

- Exhale deeply and engage your diaphragm and abdomen.

- To exit the pose, bring your legs together and bend your knees. Place your hands on the floor, and return to a seated position.

High And Low Plank Pose At The Wall

Level of difficulty: Intermediate

Focus and Intention: Arm and abdominal strength, energizing

Instructions at a glance

> NOTE: Practice the daily yoga at your wall sequence to build up strength for this pose.

- Kneel on all fours facing away from the wall. Place your hands under your shoulders and press the floor away from you. Adjust this position to accommodate the change to low plank position if necessary.

- Press your feet, one at a time, into the wall as you extend your legs behind you. Adjust the distance for your body's proportions (Figure 1).

- Firm your legs, abdomen, arms, and shoulders as you breathe deeply in high plank.

- Press your heels into the wall with vitality.

- Without changing the alignment of your body, **exhale** and lower toward the floor until your shoulders, elbows and heels form a horizontal line in the low plank position (Figure 2).

- **Do not sag in your hips or shoulders!**

- Pull your navel toward your spine.

- Perform high plank to low plank several times.

90

Tips for getting into the pose

1. If you find it challenging to go from high plank to low plank, start on your belly and lift into the low plank position.

2. Press your heels into the wall for leverage while maintaining these poses.

3. In low plank, squeeze the sides of your rib cage with your elbows.

4. **Do not** let your shoulders dip below the level of your elbows.

Exiting the pose

From high plank, return your knees to the floor and return to a seated position. From low plank, relax your belly to the floor, roll over and return to a seated position.

Yoga prop suggestions

Place your hands on yoga blocks under your shoulders.

Wrap a strap around your upper arms to hold them in place.

Suggestions for breathing in the pose

Breathe deeply into your diaphragm and feel the support from this region of your body.

Suggestion for visual focus

Focus your eyes on a point on the floor beneath you.

Imagery for alignment

Make your body as compact and strong as a wood plank. Wood doesn't sag unless it is wet, and neither should your body in this pose. Align your heels, hips, elbows, and shoulders.

"Home Play" experiments—exploring and deepening the pose

Try all the recommended variations for high and low plank in this section. Attempt the pose from the high position to the low position, and vice versa.

Experiment with the strap and feel the difference in your alignment.

When you press your head into the wall, feel the line of energy traveling from your neck down your spine into your legs.

Possible benefits and experiences of the pose

- Firms the abdomen.

- Strengthens the arms and shoulders.

- Bestows confidence and inner strength.

Precautions

- Contract and engage your abdomen to avoid strain in your lower back.

- Keep your chin away from the floor.

- Move carefully and slowly when pressing your heels or head into the wall.

High and low plank pose variation—head to the wall

  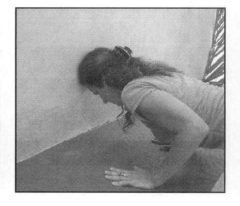

Instructions at a glance

- Follow the instructions for high or low plank pose.

- Face the wall and gently press your head into it for alignment.

- As you press your head into the wall, move your shoulders away from the wall.

High and low plank pose variation—strap around arms

Instructions at a glance

- Follow the instructions for high or low plank pose.

- Loop a yoga strap around your upper arms so they parallel each other (Figure 1).

- Readjust the strap to accommodate your body when you perform high and low plank.

- Your elbows should remain near your rib cage (Figures 3 & 4).

- Create a strong, solid line of energy from your head to your heels.

Firefly Pose At The Wall

Level of difficulty: Intermediate/Advanced

Focus and Intention: Arm and abdominal strength, hip flexibility

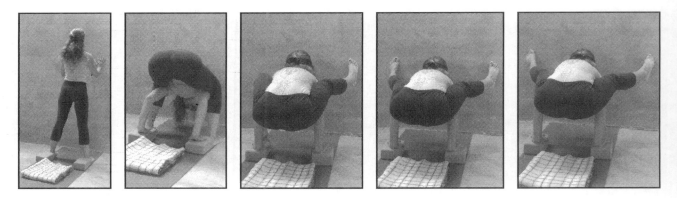

Instructions at a glance

- Place two yoga blocks about shoulder distance apart, approximately one to two feet from the wall. Your distance from the wall varies depending on your leg length.

- Place a blanket or pillow behind you (Figure 1). The blanket can ease your landing if you fall backwards on your rear end—which often happens in this pose!

- Stand in front of the blocks with your feet facing the wall (Figure 1).

- Deeply bend your knees and thread your arms inside and under your knees until you can place your hands flat on the yoga blocks, or on the floor if you don't have blocks (Figure 2).

- Bring your shoulders as far under your knees as is humanly possible.

- In one movement, drop your buttocks toward the floor behind you and simultaneously squeeze your arms with your inner thighs.

- Lift your feet off the ground toward each other, one foot at a time.

- Now extend one leg and at time and touch the wall with one foot, then the other (Figure 3).

- Continue to squeeze your arms with your legs and contract your abdominal muscles.

94

- Straighten your legs more and press the balls of your feet (Figure 4), and then your toes into the wall for leverage and balance (Figure 5).

- Exhale deeply and engage your diaphragm and abdomen.

Tips for getting into the pose

1. Focus your eyes in front of you, not behind or beneath you.

2. The more you squeeze your arms with your legs, the easier it is to lift your legs up.

3. Energize and contract from your groin to your toes as you reach toward the wall.

Exiting the pose

Bend your legs, place your feet on the floor, and stand upright. Or, sit down on the blanket behind you and release your legs from the top of your arms.

Yoga prop suggestions

Place a flat blanket behind you under your hips.

Place two yoga blocks under your hands for extra lift and ease on your wrists.

Suggestions for breathing in the pose

On your inhalations, expand your upper back. On your exhalations, contract your abdomen and squeeze your arms with your legs.

Suggestion for visual focus

Look at a point on the wall in front of you.

Imagery for alignment

When you lift your legs in this pose and are hovering in the air, imagine that you are taking flight like a firefly aglow in the night sky. Reach through your feet and legs with energy—they are your wings. Think of a radiant light emanating from your mid section.

"Home Play" experiments—exploring and deepening the pose

This pose is less intimidating than it looks. Approach it with a sense of playfulness and curiosity like a child trying a cartwheel or riding a bicycle for the first time.

Don't give up on this pose on your first try! Give your body time to figure out what is going on and what it is required to realize this pose.

Try it a few times in one yoga session, and if you don't take flight, try it again a few days later. You might be amazed at what your body has integrated with the passage of time without your efforts.

Notice the relationship between the level of activity in your abdominal muscles and your ability to lift your legs up in this pose.

Possible benefits and experiences of the pose

• Strengthens the abdominal muscles and deep hip flexors.

• Strengthens the arms.

• Encourages playfulness and confidence.

Precautions

If you feel pain in your wrists, release the pose as soon as possible. Strengthen your wrists first by practicing other poses such as downward dog, and high/low plank.

Bow/Cobra Pose Preparation At The Wall

Level of difficulty: Beginner/Intermediate

Focus and Intention: Back strength and flexibility, chest expansion, leg strength

Instructions at a glance

- Lie belly down on your yoga mat.

- Bend your knees and slide your body toward the wall until your knees/shins/tops of your feet contact the wall.

- Your knees and ankles touch or remain a few inches apart.

- Place your hands flat under your shoulders so that your **fingertips** align with the tops of your shoulders.

- Press your shoulders away from your ears and squeeze them toward your spine.

- As you press your shins into the wall, lift your chest and ribs off the floor (Figure 1).

- Utilize your back and buttocks muscles more than your arm muscles.

- Breathe deeply into your chest and upper back.

- To go deeper, lift your hips and pelvis off the floor and straighten your arms (Figure 2).

Exiting the pose

Bend your elbows and slowly lower your torso back to the floor. Slide yourself away from the wall, and return to a seated position.

Tips for getting into the pose

1. Squeeze your elbows toward your ribs when lifting into the pose.

2. Lengthen your neck.

3. Expand your chest as if your collar bone were a big smile.

Yoga prop suggestions

Place two yoga blocks under your hands for more lift.

Squeeze a yoga block between your knees or inner thighs to align and activate your legs.

Suggestions for breathing in the pose

Inhale deeply and fully as you lift into the pose. Exhale completely as you lower yourself to the floor. As you hold the pose, expand your chest and lungs as much as possible with your breath.

Suggestions for visual focus

Focus on the floor in front of you at first. As you lift higher raise your eyes to the ceiling.

Imagery for alignment

Imagine yourself as a snake slowly, silently rising from its den. Your body is languid and long. Your movements are deliberate and cautious. You have all the time in the world to peer out into the world.

"Home Play" experiments—exploring and deepening the pose

Try alternately lifting (inhale) and lowering (exhale) in this pose for 6-10 breaths, and then hold the pose.

Experiment with your hand placement. Notice any relationship between your hand placement and your ability to expand your chest and shoulders.

Remember to lift with your back and leg muscles. What happens when you use your arms to lift yourself more than your back?

Possible benefits and experiences of the pose

- Promotes flexibility in the front and back of the body.

- Increases energy and circulation.

- Strengthens the back, arms, shoulders, and legs.

- Promotes a healthy respiratory system.

- Stretches the front of your body.

Precautions

- Limit your time in this pose at the beginning if you feel discomfort in your lower back. Don't lift as high.

- Do not perform this pose if you have recently had back surgery, or open heart surgery.

Camel Pose At The Wall

Level of difficulty: Beginner/intermediate

Focus and Intention: Back strength and flexibility, chest/lung expansion

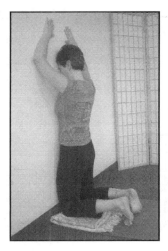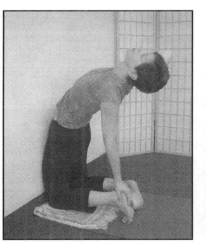

Camel variation—with Blocks

Instructions at a glance

- Kneel with your knees touching the wall on your yoga mat and/or flat blanket (Figure 1).

- Align your knees with your front hip bones.

- Press your hips and thighs into the wall by slightly contracting your buttocks.

100

- Curl your toes under (as pictured) for an easier variation, or leave the tops of your feet flat on the floor for more of a challenge.

- Bend backwards from your waist and grasp one of your heels.

- Press your shoulders away from your ears and squeeze them toward your spine.

- Cup the back of your head with your other hand as you point your elbow to the ceiling (Figure 2).

- Take a few breaths in "half camel"—the preparation for full camel. Repeat this variation on the other side.

- Release half camel pose and bring your body back to the wall.

- Now, try the pose again grasping both of your heels in full camel (Figure 3), or place your hands on yoga blocks behind your back (Figures 4 & 5).

- Firm your buttocks and press your thighs and hips into the wall.

- Breathe deeply into your chest and upper back.

- Relax your neck.

Exiting the pose

Release your heels and place your hands on your lower back. Bring your chin toward your chest, and bring your chest to the wall. Slide your knees away from the wall, and return to a kneeling or seated position.

Tips for getting into the pose

1. Lengthen your neck even though it is arched.

2. Expand your chest as if your collar bone were a big smile.

3. Firm and contract your buttocks and legs to ensure a safe and expanded backbend.

Yoga prop suggestions

Place your hands on two yoga blocks on the floor about a foot behind you.

Squeeze a yoga block between your knees or inner thighs to align and activate your legs.

Loop a yoga strap around your thighs to help maintain proper alignment.

Kneel on a blanket or knee pad.

Suggestions for breathing in the pose

As you hold the pose, expand your chest and lungs as much as possible with your breath.

Breathe through your mouth if you find it difficult to breathe through your nose.

Suggestions for visual focus

Look to the ceiling or close your eyes.

Imagery for alignment

As you arch back into half camel or camel pose, visualize a ray of light from the sun beaming down into the center of your chest. Open your heart toward that light. Breathe into that light. Let it warm your body and give you energy. You are that light.

"Home Play" experiments—exploring and deepening the pose

Practice camel in stages. First practice the pose two times with your hands on yoga blocks for about 5-7 deep breaths each time.

Then, practice the pose in the "half camel" variation on both sides cupping the back of your head.

Next, practice camel clasping your heels with toes curled under or flat on the floor.

How can you expand your chest and deepen the back bend with your breath?

When you are finished, sit your hips to your heels in child's pose and breathe into your lower back.

Possible benefits and experiences of the pose

- Promotes flexibility in the front and back of the body.

- Increases energy and circulation.

- Strengthens the back and legs.

- Promotes healthy respiratory and nervous systems.

- Expands the chest, lungs, and ribs.

Precautions

- Limit your time in this pose at the beginning if you feel discomfort in your lower back. Practice the easier variations first.

- Do not perform this pose if you have recently had heart, shoulder, or back surgery.

Wheel Pose On Blocks At The Wall

Level of difficulty: Beginner/Intermediate

Focus and Intention: Back strength and flexibility, chest expansion

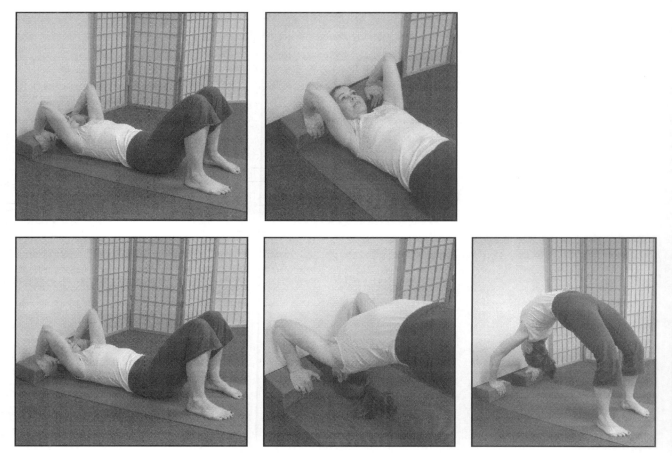

Instructions at a glance

NOTE: Since many of us typically spend many hours a day sitting or driving in a slightly forward flexed position, wheel pose is a great counter-posture to our normal pattern of movement. Physical challenges such as tight shoulders, upper back, and wrists deprive many people of the benefits of full wheel pose. Practicing wheel pose using your wall and yoga blocks can make the pose ease the pressure on your wrists, giving you extra height, and a vertical surface to push against when you lift up off the floor.

• With your yoga mat on the floor, place the yoga blocks (widest surface on the floor) against the wall a little more than your shoulder width apart.

- Lie on your back and bend your knees. Separate your feet as much as hip width apart with toes pointing straight ahead (Figure 1).

- Reach your arms up and over your head and place the palms of your hands on the yoga blocks with your fingers hanging off the edge of the block (Figure 2).

- Your head is several inches away from the wall and this distance will vary from person to person based on shoulder and back flexibility.

- Point your elbows directly toward the ceiling and depress your shoulders away from your ears.

- Engage your legs and begin to lift your hips and pelvis off the floor toward the ceiling (Figure 3).

- Press your hands into the blocks and gather strength to lift your upper body off the floor.

- Relax your neck backward and very lightly place the top of your head on the floor (Figure 4).

- Take a deep breath and simultaneously straighten your arms and lift your whole body off of the floor (Figure 5).

- Breathe deeply into your chest and upper back.

- Keep your legs and arms strong.

- Imagine you are pressing the floor away from you.

- Hold the pose for 30 seconds or longer using deep breathing through your nose (use ujjayi breathing if you are familiar with the technique).

- If you feel constriction in your throat when you breathe, release your jaw and open your mouth slightly.

Exiting the pose

Bring your chin toward your chest and bend your elbows. Slowly lower your back to the floor.

Tips for getting into the pose

1. Press and lean into your legs more than your upper body.

2. Push the blocks toward the wall for leverage.

3. Breathe through your mouth if you find it difficult to breathe through your nose.

4. Point your toes straight ahead or slightly pigeon-toed. Do not allow your knees to flop out to the sides.

5. Plant your feet into the ground.

Yoga prop suggestions

Place two yoga blocks on the floor and against the wall under your hands.

Squeeze a yoga block between your knees or inner thighs to align and activate your legs.

Loop a yoga strap around your thighs or upper arms to help maintain proper alignment.

Suggestions for breathing in the pose

Inhale deeply and fully as you lift into wheel pose. Exhale completely as you lower back to the floor. As you hold the pose, expand your chest and lungs as much as possible with your breath.

Suggestions for visual focus

Focus on the floor beneath your head. If this is too challenging, gaze at the wall.

Imagery for alignment

Visualize your body as a multi-colored rainbow as you lift and arch your spine into the sky. Where is the pot of gold, at your head or at your feet? Imagine the sun shining into your heart and enriching the many colors you embody as you hold the pose.

"Home Play" experiments—exploring and deepening the pose

Try practicing this pose 3 times in a row before hugging your legs to your knees.

After perfecting the pose against the wall with blocks, take your yoga mat to the center of your room and lift up on your own. Feel the freedom and exhilaration!

When you release the pose, feel the sensations in your whole body.

What happens when you press and lean your body weight into your legs rather than your arms? Shift your weight from your arms to your legs to find the position with the least strain, tension, or effort.

Possible benefits and experiences of the pose

- Promotes flexibility in the front and back of the body.

- Increases energy and circulation.

- Strengthens the back, arms, shoulders, and legs.

- Promotes healthy respiratory and nervous systems.

- Positively affects your spine and nervous system as you put yourself in full extension.

- Stretches the front of your body.

Precautions

- Wheel pose can be considered an inverted pose because your head position is below your heart. If you have high blood pressure, you may want to limit your time in this pose and work into it slowly and gradually.

- Limit your time in this pose at the beginning if you feel discomfort in your wrist and shoulder joints.

- Do not perform this pose if you have recently had heart, shoulder, or back surgery.

- If you feel discomfort in your lower back, do not lift as high up in the pose, and remember to keep your toes pointing forward, or turned slightly toward each other.

- *Practice cobra, upward dog, and camel pose as options if you have concerns about inverting your body.

Wheel pose variation—walking down the wall

Instructions at a glance

- Stand about one arm's length or more away from the wall (Figure 1). Adjust this position based on your back's flexibility.

- Separate your feet as much as hip width apart or wider with your toes pointing straight ahead.

- Bring your thumbs under your chin with hands in a prayer position (Figure 2).

- Push your hips forward as you reach your hands backward to the wall (Figure 3).

- Bend your knees as you walk your hands down the wall to the floor, one by one (Figure 4).

- Finally, press your hands into the floor, lean into your feet, and arch your back in the wheel pose (Figure 5).

Tips For Performing Inverted Poses

- Inverted postures should be performed with utmost care and proper alignment.

- Use blankets under your shoulders in shoulder stand, bridge formation, and plow poses.

- Make sure the blankets are FLAT!

- Utilize a flat blanket or doubled yoga mat under your head for headstands.

- Do not kick into a **headstand**. If you need to kick, it's an indication that you are improperly aligned, or have insufficient strength to perform a headstand. Build up your abdominal muscles and keep stretching your neck and shoulders first.

- Get accustomed to headstands by practicing the tri-pod headstand position without lifting your legs.

- Do not "hang-out" in a headstand with your legs **leaning** against the wall. Touch the wall with your feet periodically to help with balance and orientation.

- When the vertebrae align (because your body is strong and ready) in a headstand your feet will naturally "float" up. Trust the float principle! Levitate!

- Never perform a headstand on an unstable surface such as a bed, pillow, or cushion!

- Do not perform inverted poses immediately after eating. Wait 2-4 hours after eating before practicing inversions.

- Beginners should hold the posture for a short time (under a minute) until there is no difficulty in maintaining the pose (1 minute or more). Increase the duration gradually over time.

- When using your forearms as the base of the headstand or peacock feather pose, make sure you start out with your elbows slightly closer than shoulder width apart. Your elbows have a tendency to slide out during these poses and this causes instability.

- In a handstand pose, engage your legs, feet and inner thighs to lift upwards into the pose. Point your toes. Reach actively through your toes.

- Use the wall when first attempting the headstand, handstand, peacock feather, and scorpion poses.

- Make sure to have a firm grip on your head in supported headstand pose. When the base of the pose is solid, the pose is steady.

- Inverted poses should be followed by a resting pose until your heartbeat and breath return to normal. Child's pose is a good counter pose after headstand. After resting in child's pose, stand upright or kneel before continuing with other postures.

- Do not practice near objects or furniture.

- Don't close your eyes during a headstand. Gaze at the floor in front of you or at the edge of your yoga mat.

- If you fall out of an inversion, stay calm, and remember to keep your body relaxed.

- Use caution when practicing inversions if you have back or neck injuries, disc problems, high blood pressure, or obesity.

- Some theories suggest avoiding inversions if you have detached retina, severe narrow angle glaucoma, osteoporosis, or if you are pregnant or menstruating.

- If your eyes get bloodshot or you get broken blood vessels in your face after inverting, you may want to practice more gentle poses (downward dog, putting your legs up on a wall) until your body gets accustomed to inverting.

Shoulder Stand Pose at the Wall

Level of difficulty: Beginner/Intermediate

Focus and Intention: Back/shoulder flexibility, circulation

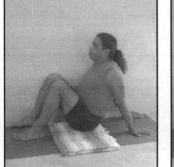    

Instructions at a glance

- Sit sideways on a flat blanket with your hip to the wall (Figure 1). Your head is OFF the blanket and shoulders are ON the blanket.

- Lean your torso backwards with arms supporting you as you swing your legs up the wall, one at a time (Figure 2).

- Scoot your hips as close to the wall as possible.

- Bend your knees and press your feet into the wall with your arms at your sides (Figure 3).

- Push your feet into the wall to lift your pelvis higher (Figure 4).

- Place your hands on your lower or mid back and wriggle your shoulders under your body (Figure 5).

- Lift your hips more.

- Remove your feet from the wall one at a time to perform the pose without the wall (not pictured).

- Relax your face, jaw, and forehead.

- Remain in this position for 10-20 breaths.

Tips for getting into the pose

1. The closer your rear end is to the wall, creating a 90 degree angle with your body, the more benefit you will receive from the posture.

2. Have your props set up or nearby before you get into the pose.

3. Your cervical vertebrae should not be crunching into the floor! Use the blanket as instructed to create space under your neck.

Exiting the pose

Lower your hips to the floor. Hug your knees to your chest. Roll over onto your right side and linger there. Press yourself back up to a seated position.

Yoga prop suggestions

Place a blanket flat under your back.

Squeeze a yoga block between your knees or inner thighs to bring strength into your legs.

Suggestions for breathing in the pose

Breathe naturally and easily through your nose. If your breath is not flowing, move your chin away from your chest. Make extra effort to keep breathing even though there is pressure on your diaphragm.

Suggestion for visual focus

Look at your toes.

Imagery for alignment

Imagine all the pressure and tension draining away from your feet and legs. All those hours of standing, walking, sitting, and working washing down your legs like water cascading down a mountainside.

"Home Play" experiments—exploring and deepening the posture

Start with 10 breaths in this pose. Then work up to 20 breaths. Make minor adjustments in your posture as you hold the pose to keep hips lifted and spine long. Ultimately, build up to 100 deep breaths.

At some point, take your feet off the wall and balance on your own. Try to achieve the same goals for remaining in the pose as you did with your feet on the wall.

When balancing on your own without the wall, it is fun and uplifting to let your legs play and explore different positions in the air.

Try out some of these variations: soles of your feet together with knees fanning open to the sides, legs in a wide open "V," one leg up/one leg down, criss-crossing the legs, and legs in a split position.

Possible benefits and experiences of the pose

- Energizes the whole body.

- Increases shoulder and back flexibility.

- Refreshes and relaxes the nervous system.

- Relieves swelling and pressure in the legs, ankles and feet.

Precautions

- Avoid dizziness by coming out of this pose slowly and gradually.

- Check with your doctor before performing this pose if you have high blood pressure or a heart condition.

- Avoid inverted poses during menstruation.

- Practice legs up the wall pose instead if you have concerns about inverting your body.

Peacock Feather Pose At The Wall

Level of difficulty: Intermediate/Advanced

Focus and Intention: Arm, shoulder and back strength, balance

Instructions at a glance

NOTE: The initial position (Figure 1) is similar to dolphin pose.

• Face the wall on your hands and knees.

• Place your elbows on the floor beneath your shoulders with your fingertips touching the wall (Figure 1), or your thumbs and index fingers framing a yoga block (Figure 2).

• Straighten your legs and lift your hips in the air.

- Press your shoulders down and create a strong foundation in your arms before you kick up.

- Reach one of your legs in the air toward the wall. Generally, if you are right-handed you will lift your left leg (Figure 3).

- Press forcefully into the floor with the lower foot to get momentum and leverage to bring that leg to the wall.

- Look to the wall or the floor between your hands.

- Let your bottom leg follow the upper leg in this movement.

- Touch the wall with both feet and point your toes (Figure 4).

- Squeeze your inner thighs together as you move your feet away from the wall to balance on your own (Figure 5). Exaggerate the upward movement by pointing your toes.

Tips for getting into the pose

1. Keep your elbows in position, shoulder width apart.

2. Keep your muscles firm like a tight glove.

3. To maintain stability and prevent slippage, wear a short sleeved shirt or roll up your sleeves so you can maintain contact between your skin and the yoga mat.

4. Draw your navel and rib cage inward.

Exiting the pose

Bring your feet back to the floor, one at a time. Bend your knees and straighten your arms. Stand upright.

Yoga prop suggestions

Press a yoga block against the wall with your thumbs and index fingers.

Place a yoga block under your lower foot to give you extra lift.

Suggestions for breathing in the poses

Direct your inhalation into your upper back and shoulders. Exhale completely and compress your abdominal region to help support your lower back.

Suggestions for visual focus

Look to the floor between your hands.

Imagery for alignment

Think about your legs being as light as a peacock feather. Feathers have a gentle curve and so does your body in this pose. Peacocks proudly display their feathers when the time is just right. Feel proud that you have attempted, or achieved, this elegant and challenging pose!

"Home Play" experiments—exploring and deepening the pose

I remember when I first tried this pose, I didn't believe my arms would actually hold me up—but they did! I experienced a rush of energy from trusting my body to take care of me. It was an exhilarating experience. I felt confident and powerful after the class.

After kicking up into this pose as described earlier, try **lifting** into it **without** kicking your leg. How do you think you will accomplish this?

Point your toes as if you wanted to touch the ceiling. Really reach your upper leg. Another trick is to put a yoga block under your bottom foot to give you some extra height.

Possible benefits and experiences of the pose

- Increases energy and circulation.

- Strengthens the arms, shoulders, and legs.

- Cultivates confidence and risk-taking.

- Strengthens the abdominal muscles.

Precautions

- If you have high blood pressure, you may want to limit your time in this pose and work into it slowly and gradually. Consult your doctor if you have doubts or questions.

- If you feel discomfort in your elbows or shoulder joints, limit your time in this pose at the beginning.

- Avoid this pose while menstruating, or after recent shoulder injuries or surgery.

- Practice dolphin or downward dog for an easier variation if you have concerns about inverting your body.

Peacock feather pose leg variations

Instructions at a glance

- Follow the instructions for getting into peacock pose.

- Bend your knees and place your feet flat on the wall (Figure 1).

- Or, cross one thigh over the other and interlace your shins and ankles (Figure 2).

- Then uncross them and do the same with the other leg.

- Stay steady and strong in your shoulders and upper back as you experiment with the leg positions.

- Are there any other leg positions you can create?

Handstand Pose At The Wall

Level of difficulty: Intermediate/Advanced

Focus and Intention: Balance, concentration, arm/shoulder strength

Handstand support with block/strap/blanket prop

Instructions at a glance

- Place your hands on the floor 4-6 inches from the wall.

- If you are trying the handstand for the first time, position the props as shown above (Figure 5 & 6).

- Your arms are strong and shoulders sturdy. Feel as if you are pushing the floor away from you.

- Extend the leg and point the toes of the foot that you will lift up to the wall.

- Put a yoga block under the bottom foot (Figure 1).

- Press your shoulders down and create a strong foundation in your arms before you reach your leg up into handstand.

- Spread your fingers.

- Reach one of your legs in the air toward the wall. Generally, if you are right-handed you will lift your left leg (Figure 2).

- Press into the floor or block with the lower foot to get leverage to bring the other leg to the wall.

- Look to the wall, or the floor between your hands.

- Let your bottom leg follow the upper leg in this movement.

- Touch the wall with both feet, point your toes and seek balance.

- Squeeze your inner thighs together as you move your feet away from the wall to balance on your own (Figure 4). Exaggerate the upward movement by pointing your toes.

Tips for getting into the pose

1. Keep your muscles firm like a tight glove.

2. Draw your navel and rib cage inward.

3. Squeeze your inner thighs together.

4. Keep your feet and toes very active.

5. Keep breathing from start to finish.

6. Stay calm and focused. Don't rush into this pose.

Exiting the pose

Bring your feet back to the floor, one at a time. Remove your hands from the floor, and stand upright.

Yoga prop suggestions

Place a yoga block under your lower foot to give you extra lift.

Tie a strap around a rolled up blanket, or use a bolster if you have one. If it is not high enough so that your head touches it, place the blanket on top of a yoga block as pictured.

Suggestions for breathing in the poses

Direct your inhalation into your upper back and shoulders. Exhale completely and compress your abdominal region to help support your lower back.

Suggestions for visual focus

Look to the floor in between your hands.

Imagery for alignment

In Sanskrit, the name for this pose is the "downward facing tree." Visualize growing roots through your hands into the Earth to connect and ground your body. Imagine that your legs are joined as one to form the strong, sturdy trunk of a tree—alive with energy.

"Home Play" experiments—exploring and deepening the pose

How does the world feel upside down? After practicing this pose for a few months, does it help you to see your life and your problems in a new way?

How do your legs feel about being free from gravity for a few minutes?

Get playful with this pose. Enjoy the freshness, energy, lightness, freedom, and liberation of being inverted. Handstand pose breaks our normal pattern of standing on our feet all day.

Possible benefits and experiences of the pose

- Increases energy and circulation.

- Encourages playfulness and freedom.

- Combats depression and fatigue.

- Strengthens the arms, shoulders, and legs.

- Cultivates confidence and risk-taking.

- Strengthens the abdominal muscles.

Precautions

- If you have high blood pressure, you may want to limit your time in this pose and work into it slowly and gradually. Consult your doctor if you have doubts or questions.

- If you feel discomfort in your wrists, elbows, or shoulder joints, limit your time in this pose and work with other poses such as downward dog and dolphin.

- Avoid this pose while menstruating, or after recent shoulder injuries or surgery.

- A little fear is normal when trying something new and daring, but don't stop breathing, and don't rush into this pose. Stay calm and focused.

- Practice downward dog and high/low plank if you have concerns about inverting your body.

Handstand pose variation—alternating split legs

Instructions at a glance

NOTE: Practice this pose only after becoming comfortable with handstand pose.

- Stand about one leg length or more from the wall and place your hands on the floor, shoulder width apart.

- Follow the main instructions and tips for lifting into handstand pose.

- Instead of joining your legs as in handstand pose, leave your legs in a split position.

- Reach your legs vigorously in opposite directions (Figure 1).

- Then, without breaking out of the handstand, keep your balance, and switch legs in mid air (Figure 2).

- Try this several times, alternating your legs in a handstand split.

- To exit the pose, bring your feet to the floor where you started, one at a time. Remove your hands from the floor, and stand upright.

Supported Headstand Pose At The Wall

Level of difficulty: Advanced

Focus and Intention: Arm, shoulder and back strength, balance, circulation

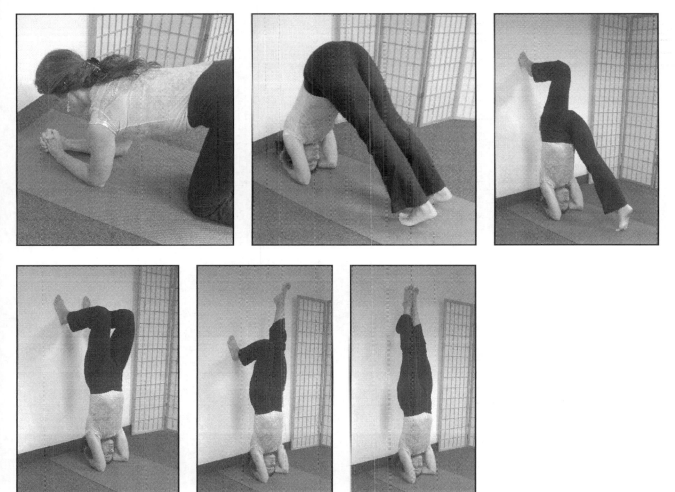

Instructions at a glance

- Start on your hands and knees, facing the wall.

- Interlace your fingers and place your hands on the floor 4-6 inches from the wall.

- Fold your yoga mat in half for extra padding under your head.

- Position your elbows directly under your shoulders. Then, move them about an inch or two closer together.

- While on your hands and knees, place the crown of your head on the floor between your interlaced hands. Your head is positioned at the top of an imaginary tripod, and your elbows are the lower two points.

- **Important: Squeeze your head tightly with your wrists and forearms.**

- Keep your neck strong and straight.

- Press your shoulders away from your ears the whole time you are in the pose.

- Straighten your legs and lift your hips in the air (Figure 2).

- Walk your feet toward your hands. As you perform this action your hips will move over your shoulders.

- Reach one of your legs up toward the wall. Keep the knee bent and touch your toes to the wall (Figure 3).

- Bring your other leg up to the wall in the same position (Figure 4).

- Slowly and carefully, straighten one leg at a time in the full headstand pose (Figure 5 & 6).

- Firm your legs, contract your abdominal muscles, point your toes, and press into your arms.

- Breathe deeply and consciously.

- Keep your eyes open and look at a point on the floor.

- Stay in the pose for a few seconds and build up to a few minutes over time.

Tips for getting into the pose

1. Keep your muscles firm like a tight glove.

2. Draw your navel and rib cage inward.

3. Squeeze your inner thighs together and firm your buttocks.

4. Keep your abdominal muscles very active.

5. Don't kick up into the pose. Reach your leg toward the wall and the other should float up to join it.

6. Stay calm and focused. Don't rush into this pose.

Exiting the pose

Bring your feet back to the floor, one at a time. Remove your head and hands from the floor, and return to a kneeling position. Rest in child's pose for at least one minute.

Yoga prop suggestions

Place yoga blocks under your feet to give you extra lift.

Place two yoga mats under your head for more comfort.

Double your yoga mat and place it under your head for more comfort.

Suggestions for breathing in the poses

Direct your inhalation into your upper back and shoulders. Exhale and compress your rib cage and abdominal region to lengthen your lower back.

Suggestions for visual focus

Look to a point on the floor in front of you.

Imagery for alignment

Think about the legs of a tripod: if one leg is out of place or shorter than the others, the tripod does not function as a tripod. The same principle applies to the poles of a tent, and also the placement of your hands/arms and head in headstand pose. If the foundation is stable and proportioned correctly, the rest of the structure functions effortlessly.

"Home Play" experiments—exploring and deepening the pose

Explore the three variations given for this pose. Which works and feels best to you?

Before you go up into the full headstand, find a spot on your head that feels just right. Your neck should not round or arch.

Experiment with ways of releasing the pose. Exit with focus, grace, and precision. Control your leg movements by regulating your breath and engaging your abdomen.

Possible benefits and experiences of the pose

- Increases energy and circulation to face.

- Combats depression and fatigue.

- Strengthens the arms, shoulders, and back.

- Cultivates confidence and risk-taking.

- Strengthens the abdominal muscles.

Precautions

- If you have high blood pressure, you may want to limit your time in this pose and work into it slowly by practicing legs up the wall pose, downward dog, and shoulder stand pose. Consult your doctor if you have doubts or questions.

- Consult with your doctor before performing this pose if you have eye, lung, or heart disease.

- If you are new to yoga, avoid this pose when pregnant.

- Avoid this pose while menstruating, or if you have shoulder or neck injuries.

- Practice downward dog, dolphin, shoulder stand, or legs up the wall first if you have concerns about inverting your body.

Headstand pose variation—tripod arm position

Instructions at a glance

- While on your hands and knees, place the very top of your head on the floor a few inches from the wall. Your head is positioned at the top of an imaginary tripod.

- Place your hands down on the bottom points of an imaginary triangle or tripod; not too close to your head.

- Your forearms should be parallel to each other and perpendicular to the floor (Figure 1).

- Keep your neck strong and straight.

- Press your shoulders away from your ears the entire time you are in the pose.

- Walk your feet toward your hands. As you perform this action your hips will lift over your shoulders.

- Separate your knees and place one knee on top of each triceps.

- Lower your feet toward your hips. Stay in this position until your legs feel like they want to levitate or float up to the ceiling. Don't panic and keep breathing!

- Keep your knees together and bent. Touch your toes to the wall (Figure 2).

- Slowly and carefully, straighten one leg at a time in the tripod headstand pose (Figure 3).

• To exit the pose, roll your legs into a ball and return to the tripod position. Or, walk your feet to the floor one at a time. Remove your head and hands and rest for at least a minute in child's pose.

Headstand pose variation facing the wall

Instructions at a glance

• Follow the main instructions for supported headstand pose.

• Remember: you'll start with your back to the wall on all fours, but you'll end up looking at the wall when you complete the pose.

• Set up the foundation of the headstand about one leg length away from the wall. Adjust the position so that your body forms an "L" shape with your feet up on the wall (Figure 2).

• Establish the base of the pose with your head and arms.

• Lift your hips up, and press your feet into the base of the wall (Figure 1).

• Walk your feet up the wall until your legs are parallel to the floor (Figure 2).

• Lift one leg in the air directly over your shoulder (Figure 3).

• Put it back onto the wall, and lift your other leg over your shoulder.

• If you are comfortable and stable, lift both legs into full headstand pose facing the wall.

• To exit the pose, walk your feet down the wall and back to the floor.

• Return to a kneeling position. Then lift your head and arms from the floor.

• Rest for at least a minute in child's pose.

Daily Yoga Sequence At The Wall

Level of difficulty: Beginner/Intermediate

Focus and Intention: Strength, flexibility, energy, general yoga "tune-up"

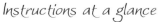
Instructions at a glance

- Stand in mountain pose facing the room; your back about a foot from the wall.

- Take a few cleansing breaths before you begin the sequence (Figure 1).

- Decide how many breaths you want to take for each pose in the sequence. I suggest starting with 5, and then as you become adept, flow through the sequence with 1 deep breath for every move. Go with the flow and don't worry if you breathe more, or less often than you intended!

- Bend your knees and sweep your arms up into chair pose with your buttocks muscles touching the wall behind you (Figure 2).

- Fold forward in front of your legs with your sit bones pressing into the wall (Figure 3).

- Push off the wall with your right foot in order to bring your left leg forward into a lunge (Figure 4 and 5).

- Bring your foot up between your hands with the knee aligned over your ankle in the runner's lunge pose. Your back heel is pressing into the wall (Figure 6).

- Sweep your arms to the side and up over your head in the arched foot warrior position (Figure 7).

- Press your right palm on the outside of your left knee and your left hand behind you into the twisting warrior position (Figure 8).

- Bring your hands down alongside your front foot and press both heels into the wall as your hips go skyward in downward dog pose (Figure 9).

- Bring your hips down toward the floor, opening your chest and keeping your legs firm and off the floor in upward dog pose (Figure 10).

- Press your hips back up into the air in downward dog again (Figure 11).

- Bring your right foot up between your hands with knee aligned over your ankle in the runner's lunge pose. Your back heel is pressing into the wall (Figure 12).

- Sweep your arms to the side and up over your head in the arched foot warrior position (Figure 13).

- Press your left palm on the outside of your right knee and your right hand behind you into the twisting warrior position (Figure 14).

- Release your hands back to the floor alongside your front foot, step your back foot forward, and fold over into the forward fold pose (Figure 15).

- Engage your legs, lift your torso, and extend your arms overhead and backward into the arching mountain pose (Figure 16).

- Return to an upright position in mountain pose (Figure 17).

- Relax your arms back to your sides in a normal standing position (not pictured).

- Step back to the wall and repeat the sequence over again as many times as you would like. You can also reverse the leg instructions and start with your right leg instead of your left leg.

Tips for performing the sequence

1. It's a little tricky to get from the forward fold pose into a lunge. It helps to press your back foot (the one not lunging forward) into the wall, and move your hands ahead of your feet.

2. Circle your arms out to the side first, and then up, when reaching your arms overhead in warrior 1 pose.

3. In the lunging and warrior poses, be sure to align your front knee directly over your ankle. If you overextend in this position, you may harm delicate knee tissue.

4. When you perform upward dog and arching mountain poses, keep the back of your neck elongated and avoid crunching your cervical vertebrae.

5. Always keep your shoulders pulled down from your ears.

Suggestions for breathing in the sequence

Generally, when you raise your arms, extend, or arch your body, the movement should be performed on your inhalation. When you contract or fold your body the movement is performed on your exhalation.

You can practice this sequence slowly by taking several breaths in each pose. You can build up to practicing this sequence more briskly, taking only one long deep breath in or out in every pose.

Suggestions for visual focus

Usually, when you are in a standing or lunging pose, look to a spot that is eye level in front of you.

While performing forward fold pose, look to your knees.

While performing downward dog pose, look to your navel center.

While performing upward dog pose, look toward the ceiling.

"Home Play" experiments—exploring and deepening in the sequence

Let the postures flow together smoothly as if you are performing a sacred dance— a movement connecting you and your body to the elements surrounding you. Become one with the essence of energy and life.

Get creative! Experiment by adding your favorite postures from other sections into the sequence mix.

133

Attempt to keep the flow going by adding poses that have a similar position or wall alignment. For example, try adding in a warrior 2 pose after warrior 1, or maybe throw in a one leg downward dog instead of a regular downward dog pose.

When you want to calm yourself, try practicing this sequence ultra slowly; feeling each and every movement.

You can practice the whole sequence with your eyes closed.

When you want to sweat a little and invigorate yourself, try practicing this sequence quickly, but without losing your form or your postural alignment.

Perform this sequence once a day, every day for one week for 10-15 minutes as soon as you rise in the morning, or anytime of the day that suits you. At week's end, reflect back on the effects the practice had on your life and your body.

Possible benefits and experiences of the posture sequence

- Warms and energizes the whole body.

- Promotes overall flexibility of the hips, spine and back.

- Strengthens the legs.

- Develops endurance and stamina.

Precautions

- Stay aware of your lower leg alignment to prevent knee strain.

- Don't over arch your back. Stay aware of your spine and pelvic alignment to prevent discomfort in your lower back.

Yoga Wall Worksheet
Create Your Own Yoga at Your Wall Sequence

Date:

Sequence Name:

1. Pose Name: Page #:

2. Pose Name: Page #:

3. Pose Name: Page #:

4. Pose Name: Page #:

5. Pose Name: Page #:

6. Pose Name: Page #:

7. Pose Name: Page #:

8. Pose Name: Page #:

9. Pose Name: Page #:

10. Pose Name: Page #:

11. Pose Name: Page #:

12. Pose Name: Page #:

13. Pose Name: Page #:

14. Pose Name: Page #:

Yoga Wall Worksheet
Create Your Own Yoga at Your Wall Sequence

Date:

Sequence Name:

    1. Pose Name: Page #:

    2. Pose Name: Page #:

    3. Pose Name: Page #:

    4. Pose Name: Page #:

    5. Pose Name: Page #:

    6. Pose Name: Page #:

    7. Pose Name: Page #:

    8. Pose Name: Page #:

    9. Pose Name: Page #:

    10. Pose Name: Page #:

    11. Pose Name: Page #:

    12. Pose Name: Page #:

    13. Pose Name: Page #:

    14. Pose Name: Page #:

Yoga Postures at Your Wall
for Balance and Steadiness

Focus on Balance and Steadiness

Balance postures cultivate awareness and require attentiveness. They establish a harmony between the upward and downward flowing energies in your body. When your mind seems scattered, life feels chaotic, or you have been very busy, you can recuperate and repose with the postures in this section. If you find it difficult to balance on one foot, allow your wall to support you in your discovery of greater levels of steadiness and mastery. As you practice, your appreciation deepens for the subtleties of attaining equilibrium.

As you practice, keep these words in mind: centeredness, presence, stillness, grace, stability, focus, integration, wholeness, acceptance, patience, concentration, attentiveness.

Specific tips for practicing the balance postures in this section:

- Perform postures for at least one minute. Your friend, the wall, will aid you in holding them longer.

- Keep breathing smoothly and steadily. If you find your breath becomes faint or short, refocus your attention on your breath—again and again. Follow the suggestions provided for breathing in each posture. Relax in the poses. Don't try so hard, and let go of internal self-pressures.

- When you feel stable in a pose, separate yourself from the wall and practice balancing on your own for part of the time.

- Practice the balance poses with your eyes open, gazing to the suggested focal point. Your visual focus greatly affects your ability to balance. Avoid letting your eyes wander.

- Practice balance poses on an even surface.

- Firm the muscles around your abdomen and navel center to enhance your ability to balance.

- Notice your thoughts while performing the yoga postures. Become aware of the affect of your thoughts on your ability to balance.

Tree Pose At The Wall (Facing Sideways)

Level of difficulty: Beginner

Focus and Intention: Balance, leg strength, stability, concentration, repose

Instructions at a glance

- Stand sideways about 2 feet away from the wall.

- Let your hand touch the wall as you explore your balance on one foot.

- Focus your eyes on a point in front of you at eye level.

- Strengthen your standing leg (the one **closest** to the wall) to be firm like a tree trunk.

- With the other leg, press your toes on the floor and turn your knee out to the side (Figure 1).

- Next, bring your foot up to the ankle area (Figure 2).

- When you are feeling more balanced, press your foot on your shin or the upper thigh of your standing leg (Figure 3). Caution: Do not press your foot into the side of your knee joint.

- Keep your hips parallel to the floor as you turn your leg further out to the side.

140

- Draw your navel toward your spine, tucking your hips, to achieve a neutral pelvic position.

- Lift your ribcage and chest. Think of a string suspended from the ceiling, tied to the bottom of your sternum, drawing your chest upward.

- Raise your arms overhead in a wide open "V" position (Figure 4) or clasped over your head with your index fingers extended (Figure 5).

- Repose in the pose and seek balance.

- Remember, you can return your hand to the wall any time lose your balance.

- Repeat the pose on the other side of your body.

Tips for getting into the pose

1. Adjust your distance from the wall so that your hand or knee can easily reach the wall and not alter the vertical alignment of your body.

2. If your shoulders are hunching or rounding forward, intensify your breath in your upper body and proudly lift your sternum.

3. Imagine your foot has 4 tires like a car and press into the areas where the tires would be. Spread your toes.

4. Relax your face and jaw line more if you find you are concentrating too hard.

Exiting the pose

Move your bent knee to a forward facing position and lower your foot to the ground. Release your arms to your sides.

Yoga prop suggestions

To become a taller tree, stand on a yoga block.

Suggestions for breathing in the pose

If you feel bottom heavy in this pose, deepen your breath in your upper chest and back. If you feel like your upper body is swaying in the wind, exaggerate your exhalations to the point of squeezing inward around your diaphragm and navel area.

Suggestion for visual focus

Look at a point eye level in front of you, or on the floor 10 to 15 feet in front of you.

Imagery for alignment

It seems silly for me to suggest that you imagine being anything other than a tree! But the type is totally up to you: Are you an umbrella pine? A noble fir? An eternal eucalyptus? A memorable mimosa? Graceful cypress? Or gracefully aging oak?

Visualize roots growing from the bottom of your feet deep into the Earth and gathering energy from the nutrients and water beneath you. With each exhalation let gravity anchor you more.

As you inhale, feel the lightness and flexibility of your upper body like delicate aspen branches whispering in the wind. Extend yourself and grow tall toward the sunlight that nourishes you.

"Home Play" experiments—exploring and deepening the posture

Feel the subtle movements and micro adjustments of your foot and ankle as you play with your balance.

Sometimes we have a tendency to hold our breath when we are concentrating too much. Pay close attention to your breath to catch yourself when you stop breathing, and begin again.

Once you are established in the pose, close your eyes and notice what it feels like to attempt to balance without a visual reference point. Let yourself yield to the feeling of being off balance. Don't try to control it!

Possible benefits and experiences of the pose

- Promotes equanimity and centeredness.

- Increases the feeling of being rooted and grounded in your body.

- Strengthens the muscles of the legs.

- Stretches the lateral hip rotator muscles.

- Creates physical and mental confidence, and reaffirms your presence on the planet.

Precautions

- To prevent knee strain, keep your big toe and knee pointing in the same direction.

- Do not press your foot into the side of your knee area.

Tree pose variation—knee to the wall as an aid to balance

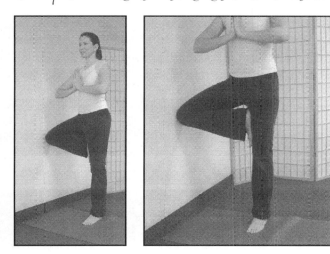

Instructions at a glance

- Stand sideways 2 feet or more away from the wall, or enough so that you can place your bent leg directly out to the side of you, perpendicular to the wall.

- Focus your eyes on a point in front of you at eye level.

- Aim to make your standing leg (the one **furthest** from the wall) firm like a tree trunk.

- Press your other foot on the shin or upper thigh of your standing leg, but not on your knee.

- Point your knee out to the side so that it touches the wall for balance.

• Draw your navel toward your spine, tucking your hips, to achieve a neutral pelvic position.

• Lift up in your rib cage and chest.

• Chose an arm position: prayer position in the center of your chest, lifted in a wide "V" position, or extended directly above your head with fingers interlaced and index fingers extended.

• Remember, you can return your hand to the wall any time lose your balance.

• Repeat the pose on the other side of your body.

Dancer's Pose At The Wall

Level of difficulty: Beginner/Intermediate

Focus and Intention: Balance, leg strength and flexibility, back flexibility

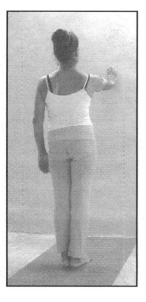   

Instructions at a glance

- Stand with your feet together, facing the wall, about one arm's length away or more.

- Bend one of your legs, reach behind you with thumb pointing down, and grab your foot or ankle with the hand on that same side.

- Using your hand on the wall to aid with balance, simultaneously lean your torso forward as you strongly press your leg and foot **away** from your back.

- Keep your hips square and point your toes.

- Keep your chest and shoulders opening up and not rounding forward.

- Attempt to take your hand off the wall and balance on your own.

- Repeat the pose on the other side of your body.

Tips for getting into the pose

1. Push your foot energetically backwards and into your hand.

2. Point your foot toward the ceiling.

3. Do **not** let your knee flare open to the side of you.

4. When you want to lean farther forward, move away from the wall, or take your hand entirely off the wall.

Exiting the pose

Lower the raised leg back to the floor and return to a standing position.

Yoga prop suggestions

If you can't reach your ankle or foot, loop a yoga strap around your foot.

Suggestions for breathing in the pose

Direct your inhalations into your upper chest and back. Focus your exhalations around the navel center.

Suggestion for visual focus

Look at a point eye level in front of you. If your torso ends up in a horizontal position, look to the floor.

Imagery for alignment

This posture is a metaphor for the human experience. Your body position in this posture points to a meaning beyond the physical. It represents our apparent condition in this life: we are in this world (the bottom foot on the Earth), but not of it (the top foot in the air).

As you push your foot away from your back, think of an archer drawing his bow ready to fire his arrow. Feel the positive tension created between your leg and your back. If your foot were released, it would shoot like an arrow from a bow.

Let your upper body take on a feeling of lightness, buoyancy and expansion. Your foot and your hand rise toward the ceiling.

"Home Play" experiments—exploring and deepening the posture

Experiment with raising your leg higher without losing your pelvic alignment.

Explore the pose by leaning your torso forward more; closer to parallel to the floor.

Challenge your back and hip muscles by squaring your hips more toward the floor or the wall (depending on the angle of your torso).

Try flexing your foot, then pointing your toes, and feel which muscles are activated with this slight change of form.

Try holding your foot/ankle on the inside with your thumb pointing up. Notice any different sensations of stretching in your arm, shoulder, or chest.

Possible benefits and experiences of the pose

- Promotes leg, shoulder and back flexibility.

- Increases chest and lung expansion.

- Stretches the quadriceps muscles of the legs.

- Strengthens the hamstrings and gluteus muscles.

Precautions

Keep your knees and toes in alignment to prevent knee strain.

Dancer's pose variation—classic position

Instructions at a glance

- Symbolism: Life's mysteries and truths are at times revealed to us in those "ah-ha" moments (symbolized by the upper palm open and exposed), and at other times concealed from us (symbolized by the lower palm facing inward and unexposed).

- Stand at a slight diagonal about a foot away from your wall, or far enough so that when you bend your knee, your hip lightly touches the wall.

- Turn out the foot closest to the wall at about a 45° angle or more, and slightly bend your leg.

- Lift your other leg to about the height of your hips with the knee bent and toes pointed.
- Raise your arms into the positions shown in the photos.

- Bend your index finger until the fingertip touches your thumb tip. This is a hand symbol (called "Mudra" in Sanskrit) signifying the intent for our ego to surrender to our higher self.

- Draw your navel toward your lower back, tucking your hips for a neutral pelvic position.

- Experiment with deepening the bend in your standing leg and/or lifting the upper leg higher.

- Balance in this posture feeling the upward- and downward-moving forces in your legs.

- Focus on a point at about eye level in front of you and continue to breathe deeply.

- To exit the pose, relax your arms and lower your leg to the floor.

- Repeat the pose on the other side of your body.

Warrior 3 At The Wall

Level of difficulty: Intermediate

Focus and Intention: Leg and back strength, stability, balance

Instructions at a glance

- Face the wall from about the distance of one leg's length.

- Measure the approximate distance for this pose by raising one of your legs up and pressing your foot/ball of your foot into the wall (Figure 1).

- Remove your foot from the wall and join your feet together. From where you are standing, turn to face away from the wall.

- Like a see-saw, lean your torso forward into a horizontal position, and at the same time lift your back leg up in the air level with your torso.

- Press your foot into the wall and straighten your leg, toes pointing downward. If you cannot fully straighten your leg, readjust your position.

- Bring your hands to your waist (Figure 2) and then extend your arms alongside your body (Figure 3).

- Both of your frontal hip bones should face the floor (a.k.a. squaring your hips).

- Drop your shoulders down away from your ears.

- Keep contracting your abdominal muscles toward your back.

- Breathe deeply as you intentionally elongate your body from your foot to the top of your head.

- Repeat the pose on the other side of your body.

Tips for getting into the pose

1. Actively push your foot backwards and into the wall.

2. Keep your abdominal muscles moving toward your back.

3. Square your hips. Keep your frontal hip bones facing the floor. Do not let your knee and foot of the back leg turn out.

4. Lengthen the back of your neck.

Exiting the pose

Lower the raised leg back to the floor and return to a standing position.

Yoga prop suggestions

The wall is your best prop for this pose.

Suggestions for breathing in the pose

On your exhalation, activate your abdominal muscles and expel all the air from your lungs.

Suggestion for visual focus

Look at a point on the floor below you.

Imagery for alignment

If this pose tends to feel a bit heavy in the legs and lower body, imagine something light, like a feather or leaf, as you practice.

You can also imagine that your body forms an arrow, and the direction of current is traveling from your foot toward your head and out into the space of the room.

"Home Play" experiments—exploring and deepening the posture

Vary the position of your arms: out to the side like you are flying, or overhead like Superman. Notice the changes in sensations and the shifts in your ability to balance.

Possible benefits and experiences of the pose

- Promotes leg and back strength.

- Strengthens the hamstrings and gluteus muscles.

- Encourages determination and confidence.

Precautions

- Keep your knees and toes in alignment to prevent knee strain; especially in the standing leg.

- Slightly bend the knee of your standing leg if you feel discomfort or you have a tendency to hyperextend your knee joints.

- Move slowly and consciously when attempting to press your foot into the wall.

Warrior 3 variation—arms pressing the wall overhead

Instructions at a glance

- Face the wall about the distance of one leg's length.

- Like a see-saw, lean your torso forward into a horizontal position. At the same time, lift your back leg to the level to your torso.

- This back leg is very active, as if you were kicking something behind you.

- Extend your arms over head and press your hands into the wall.

- Both of your frontal hip bones should face the floor (a.k.a. squaring your hips).

- Drop your shoulders down from your ears.

- Continue to contract your abdominal muscles toward your back.

Half Moon 2 Pose With Back To The Wall

Level of difficulty: Beginner/Intermediate

Focus and Intention: Balance, expansion, leg strength, shoulder stretch

Instructions at a glance

- If you are using a yoga block, place it next to the wall, about a foot or more in front of the toe tips of your right foot.

- Stand about 4-7 inches from the wall with your legs spread about one leg length apart (Figure 1).

- Turn your right foot forward, parallel to the wall.

- Bend your right knee and look down.

- Place your fingertips or hand on the floor, or on the yoga block near the wall (Figure 1).

- Energetically lift your left leg up in the air until it is parallel to the floor (Figure 2).

- Flex your left foot and keep the leg in the air firm and actively engaged.

- Straighten your standing leg, inviting your quadriceps to be strong and solid.

- Look toward the floor until you feel balanced.

- Rolling your torso open, lean your shoulders, arms and hips into the wall. Right arm is in alignment with your lower arm (Figure 3).

- Send the energy from your core to into your limbs.

- Turning your head, focus your eyes on a point on the ceiling, or the thumb of your hand that is above you.

- Let the wall support you, and keep your legs full of life.

- Breathe deeply and expand into your finger tips and feet.

- Repeat the pose on the other side of your body.

Tips for getting into the pose

1. If you sense discomfort in your knee, bend your standing leg slightly.

2. Your lower hand should be nearer to the wall than your standing leg.

3. Align your head and neck with your spine.

4. Let your heart area lead the way by moving your head backwards a bit.

Exiting the pose

Bend your standing leg and lower your upper leg to the floor as you return to a standing position.

Yoga prop suggestions

Place one or two yoga blocks under your hand with the widest side of the block on the floor.

Suggestions for breathing in the pose

If the pose becomes more challenging, maintain an even and smooth breathing pattern. On your out breaths, firm the region from your diaphragm to your navel. On your in breaths, feel the expansion and movement of your breath into your upper chest and upper back.

Suggestion for visual focus

First, focus on a point on the floor.

When you have established your balance, look to a point in front of you. Then, look at a point on the ceiling, or to your thumbnail (if your arm is in the air).

Imagery for alignment

Imagine your body is a half moon floating in the night sky. Create a strong and long line from your foot to the top of your head. Let the wall steady you as you experiment with liberating and opening your body.

"Home Play" experiments—exploring and deepening the posture

Experiment with the hand placement of your lower hand. Ar first, place your fingertips on a yoga block or two for maxium lift and height. Then, progress to placing your palm flat on the block. From there, you can move the block away and repeat these steps with your hand touching the floor.

Explore the position of your upper leg by lifting it more into the air, or lowering it toward the floor. Finally, find a spot where you feel your hips expanding and your leg muscles firming at the same time.

Possible benefits and experiences of the pose

- Promotes openness and expansion in the chest and shoulders.

- Strengthens the quadriceps and the legs.

- Cultivates balance and freedom of movement.

Precautions

- Keep your knee and big toe aligned to prevent knee strain.

- Slightly bend your standing leg if you have a tendency to hyperextend in your knee joints.

Half Moon 2 Pose With Foot To The Wall

Level of difficulty: Beginner/Intermediate

Focus and Intention: Balance, expansion, leg strength, chest opening

Instructions at a glance

- Standing with your side toward the wall, raise your arm to shoulder level and reach for the wall with your fingertips barely touching (Figure 1).

- From here, turn your right foot to point away from the wall.

- Place your fingertips (or hand) on the floor (or on a yoga block), about one foot in front and slightly to the outside of your right foot (Figure 2).

- Bend your knees slightly before you lift your left leg.

- Lift your left leg until it is parallel to the floor (Figure 3).

- Press your foot into the wall with the arch of your foot parallel to the floor.

- Look toward the floor until you feel balanced.

- Bring your left hand to your hip, expanding your chest and torso (Figure 4).

- Raise your left arm toward the ceiling and extend your head and your limbs from your core like a starfish (Figure 5).

- Turn your head and focus on a point on the ceiling.

- Reverse your body to perform the pose on the other side. Don't forget to move the block.

Tips for getting into the pose

1. You may want to paint or stencil a few of your favorite yoga designs on the ceiling to provide you with an appealing spot to focus on during your practice.

2. Your leg is in the correct position when you can press the whole sole of your foot into the wall, and comfortably straighten your leg. You may have to measure a few times before you find the perfect distance for your body.

3. Move slowly and consciously when pressing your foot into the wall.

4. Align your head and neck with your spine. Let your heart area lead the way by moving your head backwards.

5. Keep the knee of your standing leg slightly flexed to activate the quadriceps muscles and avoid hyperextension.

Exiting the pose

Bending your knees slightly, remove your foot from the wall.

Lower your arm, and carefully return to a standing position.

Yoga prop suggestions

Place one or two yoga blocks on the floor under your hand for extra lift and support.

Suggestions for breathing in the pose

On your exhalations, tighten and firm from your diaphragm to your navel.

On your inhalations, feel the expansion and the movement of your breath into your chest and shoulders.

Suggestions for visual focus

First, focus on a point on the floor.

When you have established your balance, look to a point in front of you. Then, look to a point on the ceiling or at your thumbnail (if your arm is in the air).

Imagery for alignment

Imagine you are a luminous starfish. Feel your navel as the center, and your limbs and head are bright lasers of light illuminating all 5 directions. Exhale, and the light renews itself at your core. Inhale, and the light radiates and brightens the room.

"Home Play" experiments—exploring and deepening the posture

When you practice this posture, move your torso and upper body further backward into space as if you were a starfish freely floating in the ocean. Be sure to keep your foot pressed into the wall for stability.

Experiment with your shoulder and arm position to achieve a feeling of maximum openness for your chest and upper back.

Tilt your pelvis a little forward, then a little backward, until you discover a position of stability in your lower body.

Possible benefits and experiences of the pose

- Strengthens the quadriceps, legs and hips.

- The wall aids your balance and maintains your stability in this pose.

- The wall encourages expansion, empowerment and risk taking.

Precautions

- Awareness of your lower leg alignment prevents knee strain.

- Avoid knee discomfort by keeping your standing leg slightly bent.

- Turning your head too quickly may create dizziness and imbalance.

Eagle Pose At The Wall

Level of difficulty: Beginner/Intermediate

Focus and Intention: Leg strength and flexibility, balance, bringing energy
                          toward the midline of your body

Instructions at a glance

- Stand with your feet together about one foot or so from your wall, or close enough for your backside to touch when you bend your knees.

- Bend your knees as if you were about to sit back into a chair.

- Cross your left leg tightly over the right (or vice versa) at the inner thigh region.

- First, the foot of your crossed leg contacts the yoga block (Figure 1) or the floor.

- Now, bring your elbows up to shoulder height and cross the right over the left (the **opposite movement** from what the legs are doing).

- One hand will now be lower than the other. With palms **facing** each other, reach the bottom hand up to hold part of the upper hand (you may only reach the base of the thumb).

- Lower your elbows toward your ribcage as you actively squeeze them together.

- If your legs feel flexible, wrap the foot of the crossed leg behind the ankle or shin of your standing leg (Figure 2).

- Continue to bend your knees and squeeze together your inner thighs and elbows as you deepen the pose.

- Drop your shoulders down, away from your ears.

- Soften your facial and jaw muscles as you look at a point at eye level in front of you.

- Draw your navel toward your lower back and tuck your hips, achieving a neutral pelvic position.

- Repeat the pose on the other side of your body.

Tips for getting into the pose

1. Bend your standing leg a little more, if you find it challenging to wrap your foot behind your ankle/shin.

2. If/when the movement of crossing your elbows is too challenging, wrap your arms around your upper chest and hug yourself instead.

3. If/when the movement of crossing your knees is too challenging, keep your knees together and bend them as if you were sitting on a chair.

Exiting the pose

Lower the crossed leg back to the floor, unbraid your arms, and return to a regular standing position.

Yoga prop suggestions

Place one or two yoga blocks beside your standing leg to raise the floor to the foot of your crossing leg.

Suggestions for breathing in the pose

Extend your breath into your upper back, shoulder blades and collarbone on your inhalations. On your exhalations, squeeze your arms and legs together.

Suggestion for visual focus

Look at an eye level point in front of you. If your hands are in the way, look to one side of your hands to a point on the floor out in front of you.

Imagery for alignment

Imagine that you are a boa constrictor, wrapping around yourself. Feel the pulsation of your energy contracting and expanding. Draw your breath and energy toward the center and midline of your body.

"Home Play" experiments—exploring and deepening the posture

Experiment with slowly moving your arms up or down. Feel the different sensations occuring in your chest, arms and upper shoulders with these motions.

Explore the pose by leaning your torso forward more; almost parellel to the floor, like an eagle pointing its beak down as it scans the ground for prey.

Possible benefits and experiences of the pose

- Promotes shoulder, arm and upper back flexibility.

- Strengthens the muscles of your inner thighs, quadriceps and chest.

- Stretches the ankles.

Precautions

Don't force your ankles, arms or wrists into the wrapped positions.

Standing Leg Extension Pose At The Wall

Level of difficulty: Beginner/Intermediate

Focus and Intention: Leg and hip strength and flexibility, balance

Instructions at a glance

- Stand with your feet together and toes pointing straight ahead about 3-6 inches from the wall. Allow enough space for your backside to contact the wall and to lift your leg.

- Bend your knee as you lift your right thigh toward your torso.

- Lean a little forward to hook your index and second fingers around the inside of your big toe (Figure 1).

- Hold your toe firmly as you straighten (as much as possible) your leg in front of you (Figure 2).

- Let the wall support you to balance more easily in this position.

- Keep your spine straight and abdominal muscles engaged.

- Rotating your hip, move your leg to your right side.

- Draw your navel toward your lower back and tuck your hips, achieving a neutral pelvic position.

- Preserve the strength in your standing leg.

- Focus your gaze on a point at eye level in front of you.

- Repeat the pose on the other side of your body.

Tips for getting into the pose

1. Curl your toes away from your fingers as if they were trying to escape from your grip.

2. Lengthen your spine. Avoid hunching or leaning forward.

3. Your raised leg need not straighten completely.

4. If it feels uncomfortable to hold your big toe, hold the outside of your foot or the inside of your heel.

5. Lift your leg with your arm strength until your leg gets stronger.

Exiting the pose

Return your leg to the extended position in front of you, bend the knee, and release the toe or foot hold. Lower your leg back to the floor, returning to a standing position.

Yoga prop suggestions

If you can't reach your ankle or foot, loop the yoga strap over the ball of your foot and hold both ends in the hand nearest your foot.

Suggestions for breathing in the pose

Deepen your inhalations as you lift your leg with the intention of keeping your spine erect.

Suggestion for visual focus

Look at a point at eye level in front of you.

Imagery for alignment

As you lift your leg in the air, imagine that the strength of it can levitate the rest of your body off the floor. Entertain the notion that you can hover a bit above the ground.

"Home Play" experiments—exploring and deepening the posture

Experiment with raising or lowering your leg to find the perfect alignment for you at this moment.

Lift the top of your head toward the ceiling as you anchor into your foot. Experience the opposing forces in this posture.

Extend your back and spine more and more without leaning too far backwards.

Explore the pose, drawing your chest toward your thigh, or chin toward your knee in front of you. You may need to increase your distance from the wall to accomplish this variation.

Possible benefits and experiences of the pose

- Promotes leg and hip flexibility.

- Encourages good posture.

- Stretches the back of the legs and hip rotators.

- Strengthens leg and abdominal muscles.

- Increases a sense of balance and stability.

Precautions

- Keep your knees and toes in alignment to prevent knee strain.

- Keep your knees slightly bent if you have a tendency to hyperextend them.

Leg extension variation—with yoga strap

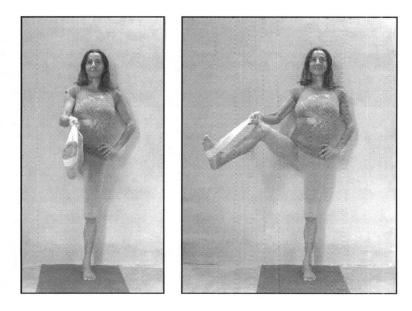

Instructions at a glance

• Make a loop with the yoga strap and hook it around the arch or ball of your foot.

• Follow the main instructions for performing this pose, substituting the strap for the actions of your hand.

Leg extension variation—foot press facing the wall

Instructions at a glance

• Stand with your feet together, facing the wall, about one leg's length away.

• Place your hands on your waist or hips.

• Lift and bend one of your legs, then straighten it and press the bottom of your foot into the wall so that it parallels the floor.

• Elongate and lift your spine and back.

• Press your foot into the wall.

• Keep your hips level.

• Repeat the pose on the other side of your body.

Standing Leg Extension Twist Pose At The Wall

Level of difficulty: Intermediate

Focus and Intention: Leg strength, leg, spine and shoulder flexibility,
                          stimulating internal organs

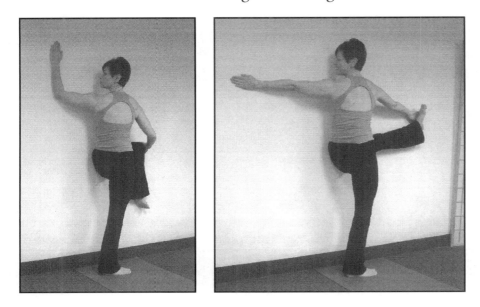

Instructions at a glance

- Stand sideways about 2-4 inches from the wall with your feet together and toes pointing straight ahead, or enough so that the side of your hip contacts the wall.

- Bend and lift the leg closest to the wall, and then hold the knee with your **opposite** hand (Figure 1).

- From the navel up, turn to face the wall (Figure 1).

- Hug the wall with your free arm.

- Reach down and hold the **outside** of your foot.

- Straighten your leg (as much as possible) in front of you (Figure 2).

- Allow the wall to support you to enhance your balance.

- Twist deeply toward the wall as you reach with your arms.

- Keep your spine upright and abdominal muscles active.

- Draw your navel toward your lower back, tucking your hips, to achieve a neutral pelvic position.

- Maintain your frontal hip bones in a forward position.

- Focus your gaze on the thumbnail of your back hand.

- Reverse your direction and repeat the pose on the other side of your body.

Tips for getting into the pose

1. Push your foot into your hand as if it were trying to escape from your grip.

2. Reach actively through your arms from hand to hand.

3. If you want to balance on your own, shift your weight into the standing leg. Or, simply position yourself farther away from the wall when you initiate the posture.

Exiting the pose

Bend your knee and lower the raised leg to the floor, untwist, and return to a standing position.

Yoga prop suggestions

If you can't reach your ankle or foot, use a yoga strap with one end in a loop, and wrap it around the ball of your foot.

Suggestions for breathing in the pose

Focus your inhalations in your upper chest and back as you lift and elongate your body. Intensify your exhalations in your diaphragm area with every twist.

Suggestion for visual focus

Look at a point eye level in front of you as you lift your leg. As you twist, look to the thumbnail of your back hand.

Imagery for alignment

Hug the wall. Let the wall support you like the embrace of a trusted friend.

"Home Play" experiments—exploring and deepening the posture

Experiment with raising your leg.

Use your foot hold as the point of contact for gaining leverage in the twist.

Challenge your lower body by maintaining pelvic stability as you deepen the twist in your upper body.

Possible benefits and experiences of the pose

• Promotes leg, shoulder and spinal flexibility.

• Expands the chest and lung.

Precautions

• To prevent knee strain, maintain the alignment between your knees and toes.

• To prevent lower back strain, twist upward from the navel.

Yoga Wall Worksheet

Create Your Own Yoga at Your Wall Sequence

Date:

Sequence Name:

    1. Pose Name: Page #:

    2. Pose Name: Page #:

    3. Pose Name: Page #:

    4. Pose Name: Page #:

    5. Pose Name: Page #:

    6. Pose Name: Page #:

    7. Pose Name: Page #:

    8. Pose Name: Page #:

    9. Pose Name: Page #:

    10. Pose Name: Page #:

    11. Pose Name: Page #:

    12. Pose Name: Page #:

    13. Pose Name: Page #:

    14. Pose Name: Page #:

Yoga Postures at Your Wall
for Flexibility and Expansion

Focus on Flexibility and Expansion

It takes time for lifelong patterns to be reversed. Our bodies acquire certain feelings and form based on the repetitive movements we make—conscious or unconscious. How we sit, stand, sleep, eat and walk all affect our posture and physical holding patterns. If you assume a "hurry up and relax" attitude with these yoga postures, you will create more tension than relaxation.

This section focuses on ameliorating the effects of years of habits, patterns, and movement you have experienced in your body. Take extra time, and be extra patient with your body when introducing these postures to your practice; perhaps even more than the postures in the other sections. Remember, it took you a long time to accumulate the tensions and it may take a while to undo what has been done.

Deep, slow rhythmic breathing has been shown to contribute to a greater relaxation response and parasympathetic input. We physically relax in response to the signals our brain and nervous system (and other systems as well) are sending throughout our bodies. Our brain communicates via a system of proprioceptors, or nerve endings, in muscles, tendons and joints. Breathing deeply and slowly is of the utmost importance while performing the poses in this section.

As you practice, keep these words in mind: unfold, undo, unwind, unravel, melt, surrender, soften, lengthen, elongate, stretch and relax.

Specific tips for practicing the postures in this section:

- To allow time for release and relaxation, perform each posture for at least one minute or longer.

- Warm up with a light sweat before starting the flexibility practices. Jog in place, jump up and down, ride your bike, do a few jumping jacks or practice the shake and breathe technique described in section 1.

- Extend your exhalations to intentionally deepen your relaxation as you breathe out.

Forearm Press At The Wall

Level of difficulty: Beginner
Focus and Intention: Arm, chest, shoulder, and back stretch

Instructions at a glance

- Stand about 2 feet from the wall and press the backs of your forearms against the wall, higher than your shoulders (Figure 1).

- Walk backwards as you let your chest and torso relax toward the floor.

- Keep your forearms parallel to each other and avoid letting your elbows slip out to the sides as you go deeper.

- Keep your spine long and tail bone tucked slightly to avoid the tendency of over arching your lower back.

- Breathe deeply, allowing your chest and shoulders to relax more with each exhalation.

- For a slightly different stretch, lift your elbows off the wall with only your palms in contact with the wall (Figure 2).

Tips for getting into the pose

1. Keep your legs slightly bent if you feel discomfort in your knees.

2. Spread your fingers as wide apart as possible.

3. Keep your arms parallel to each other. Don't let your elbows slide apart.

4. Align your head and neck with your spine. Let your heart area melt towards the Earth.

5. Avoid scrunching up your shoulders. Keep your shoulders down, away from your ears.

Exiting the pose

Walk toward the wall and let your arms fall to your sides. Return to a standing position.

Yoga prop suggestions

Place yoga block between your inner knees or upper thighs to activate your legs and maintain your leg alignment.

Suggestions for breathing in the pose

Inhale slowly as if you were trying to gradually fill your lungs all the way up to your collar bone and shoulder blades.

Suggestion for visual focus

Let your eyes focus on a point on the wall. As you go deeper into the posture, look to a point on the floor underneath you.

Imagery for alignment

Imagine your armpits are yawning toward the wall. Your body creates a comma, a pause in the sentence of your life. As you allow your heart to release toward the floor, allow love and well-being to enter your body.

"Home Play" experiments—exploring and deepening the posture

Experiment with your hand and forearm placement. Raise your arms higher on the wall, then notice the effects the shift has on your body. Bring your arms closer together, then farther apart. Find the position that feels just right for you in this moment; not too much, not too little sensation.

Take your elbows off the wall and straighten your arms. Notice any new sensations in your arms and back.

Possible benefits and experiences of the pose

- Promotes openness and expansion in the chest and shoulders.

- Stretches the muscles of the arms, upper back and shoulder girdle.

- Cultivates greater range of motion in the shoulders.

- Releases shoulder tension and stress.

Precautions

Keep your spine straight and strong to prevent over arching your lower back.

Slightly bend your legs if you have a tendency to hyperextend in your knee joints.

"Arm Clock" Shoulder Stretch At The Wall

Level of difficulty: Beginner
Focus and Intention: Shoulder and arm flexibility

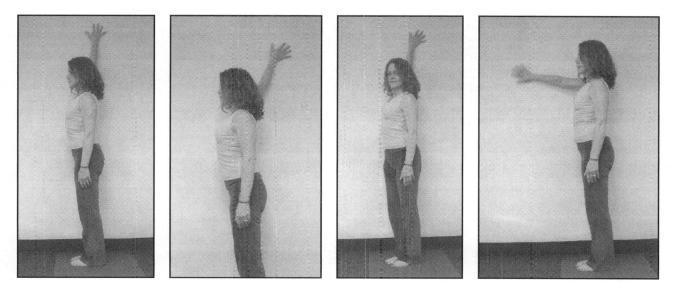

Instructions at a glance

- Stand sideways with your feet together, a few inches from the wall. If your shoulders are tight, you may have to increase your distance from the wall.

- Raise your arm closest to the wall to the imaginary point of 12 o'clock (Figure 1).

- Spread your fingers; straighten your arm, lifting your elbow OFF the wall.

- Keep your palm pressing firmly into the wall.

- From there, slowly move your hand backwards to the imaginary points of 1 or 2 o'clock if it is your right arm, and towards 11 or 10 o'clock if it is your left arm (Figure 2).

- Be gentle with this movement so as not to damage your rotator cuff.

- Walk your hand back more if you want to do deeper, but do so **without** arching your back.

- Move your feet to point away from the wall to increase the stretch (Figure 3).

• When you finish the pose, turn your feet forward and slowly release your arm in front of you.

• Notice the sensations in your arms when you complete the pose (Figure 4).

• Repeat the pose on the other arm.

Tips for getting into the pose

1. Press your shoulders actively down from your ears.

2. Spread your fingers as wide apart as possible.

3. Move your whole arm backward, not just your hand or wrist.

4. Let your heart area melt towards the Earth.

Exiting the pose

Allow your arm to return to your side.

Yoga prop suggestions

Place a yoga block between your inner knees or upper thighs to help activate your legs and maintain your leg alignment.

Suggestions for breathing in the pose

Inhale slowly as if you were trying to gradually inflate your entire lungs from the diaphragm all the way up into the armpit. When you exhale, relax your shoulders more.

Suggestion for visual focus

Focus on a point eye level in front of you as you move through the positions.

Imagery for alignment

Imagine your raised arm is the big hand on a clock. Move your arm as one unit, as slowly as time moves, from minute to minute. Take your time and let your shoulder tension release with each minute and deep breath.

"Home Play" experiments—exploring and deepening the posture

Experiment with your arm placement on the face of the clock.

Raise your elbow higher off the wall and notice the effects.

Relax your shoulders if you become aware of them hunching.

Press your palm more firmly into the wall.

As you walk your feet away from the wall, notice any new sensations in your arms and back.

After you release your arm take a look in the mirror. Does your stretched arm look longer than the other one?

Possible benefits and experiences of the pose

- Promotes openness and expansion in the chest and shoulders.

- Stretches the muscles of the arms, upper back and shoulder girdle.

- Cultivates greater range of motion in the shoulders.

- Releases shoulder tension and stress.

Precautions

- Keep your spine straight and strong to prevent over arching in the low back.

- If your elbows hyperextend, keep a slight bend in your elbow and do not straighten your arm all the way.

- It is not healthy to over stretch your joints. Don't force your arm to reach further behind you than is comfortable.

"Hitchhiker" Arm Stretch Pose At The Wall

Level of difficulty: Beginner

Focus and Intention: Arm, chest, and shoulder stretch

 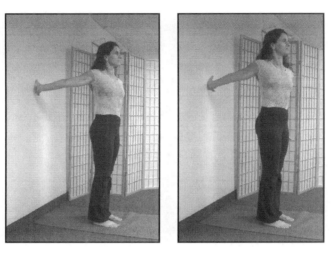

Instructions at a glance

- Stand facing away from the wall with your feet together, your arm's distance from the wall. If your shoulders are tight, you may have to **decrease** your distance from the wall.

- Keep your chest and hips pointing forward as you hold the position and breathe.

- Raise your arm out to the side of you to shoulder height, if possible. Like a hitchhiker, point your thumb up to the ceiling (Figure 1).

- Spread your fingers. Touch your fingertips to the wall behind you. If you feel a stretching sensation in your arm, you don't need to go any further.

- From there, slowly move your hand backwards until your palm is pressing flat against the wall. Step backward if you cannot fully flatten your palm (Figure 2).

- Inch your hand back more if you want to go deeper into the posture, but do so **without** arching your back (Figure 3).

- Repeat the pose on the other arm.

Tips for getting into the pose

1. Pressing your shoulders actively down from your ears.

2. Spread your fingers as wide apart as possible.

Exiting the pose

Allow your arm to return to your side.

Yoga prop suggestions

Place a yoga block between your inner knees or upper thighs to activate your legs and maintain your leg alignment.

Suggestions for breathing in the pose

Inhale slowly as if you were breathing into and toward your fingertips. When you exhale, relax your shoulders more.

Suggestion for visual focus

Focus on a point eye level in front of you as you move through the arm positions.

Imagery for alignment

Visualize an elastic band stretching from your wrist to the center of your chest. With each inhale the band gets longer.

"Home Play" experiments—exploring and deepening the posture

Experiment with your hand placement. Place your hand higher or lower on the wall.

Relax your shoulders if you become aware of them hunching. Stay conscious of your breath and breathe constantly throughout the pose.

Press your palm more - or less - firmly into the wall. Become aware of your reactions if the sensations become too intense. Do you push yourself? Do you retreat at the slighest discomfort? What are you afraid of?

Possible benefits and experiences of the pose

- Promotes openness and expansion in the chest and shoulders.

- Stretches the muscles of the arms and shoulder girdle.

- Cultivates greater range of motion in the shoulders and wrists.

Precautions

- Keep your spine straight and strong to prevent over arching in the lower back.

- If your elbows hyperextend, keep a slight bend in your elbow and do not straighten your arm all the way.

- Always be aware of your rotator cuff and do not push past your shoulder comfort. It is not healthy to over stretch your joints. Don't force your arm to reach further behind you than is comfortable.

Half Moon 1 Pose At The Wall

Level of difficulty: Beginner
Focus and Intention: Side body and shoulder stretch

Instructions at a glance

- Stand sideways a few inches from the wall with your hip touching the wall.

- Raise your arms overhead with your palms facing the ceiling.

- Grab the wrist of the hand that is closest to the wall and pull upward. A gentle stretch extends from your wrist, down your side, down your leg to your foot.

- Lift your ribs away from your hips and lean to the side until you feel the stretch in the side of your body closest to the wall (Figure 1).

- After holding the pose for a minute or more, return to an upright position keeping your arms overhead and your hands in the **same position**.

- Step about a foot or more from the wall, bend at the waist, and lean toward the wall.

- Press your hand to the wall and lean into the side stretch on this side (Figure 2).

- Move your hips away from the wall, using the wall as leverage as you push yourself into a deeper stretch.

• Turn around and repeat both positions on the other side of your body.

Tips for getting into the pose

1. Press your shoulders down, away from your ears.

2. Lean directly to the side.

3. Avoid collapsing your arms or chest forward.

4. Keep lengthening your lower back by slightly tipping your pelvis under and firming your buttocks muscles.

Exiting the pose

When you have performed the pose on both sides, stand up straight and release your arms to your sides.

Yoga prop suggestions

Place a yoga block between your inner knees or upper thighs to activate your legs and maintain your leg alignment.

Suggestions for breathing in the pose

On your inhalations, feel as if you are growing taller. On your exhalations, relax deeply into the side stretch.

Suggestion for visual focus

Let your eyes focus on a point eye level in front of you.

Imagery for alignment

Imagine you are a crescent moon hanging in the night sky. Allow yourself to delight in the smooth arch your body is making.

"Home Play" experiments—exploring and deepening the posture

Turn your head and look toward the ceiling. Point the elbow of your upper arm toward the ceiling as you expand your armpit area. Does this change the experience of the posture?

Now rest your head on the bicep of your bottom arm. How does this change the pose?

If your shoulders begin to hunch, relax them.

Press your palm more - or less - firmly into the wall.

Possible benefits and experiences of the pose

• Promotes openness and expansion in the waist, ribs, and sides of your body.

• Stretches the muscles of the arms and shoulders.

• Strengthens your arms and wrists.

Precautions

If you notice that your chest and upper body collapses forward, you may be over stretching in this posture.

Half moon 1 variation—on the floor

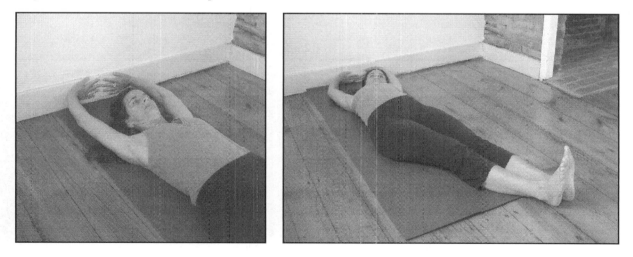

Instructions at a glance

- Lie flat on your back with your feet together and arms reaching overhead, palms facing the ceiling.

- Adjust your position if you do not have enough room to straighten your arms.

- Press your hands into the wall and press your shoulders down and toward the floor.

- Move your legs, one at a time, out to one side. At the point of maximum stretch, press the arches of your feet together. If you have gone too far you may notice one of your palms lifting off the wall.

- Squeeze your inner thighs together, and keep your buttocks and shoulders in contact with the floor.

- Return your legs to the center position and repeat the pose on the other side.

Torso Rotation Pose At The Wall

Level of difficulty: Intermediate
Focus and Intention: Side body and shoulder stretch

Instructions at a glance

- Stand sideways a few feet from the wall.

- Place your hand on the wall with your elbow bent (Figure 1).

- Press the foot closest to the wall into your upper inner thigh (Figure 2).

- Raise your free arm up in the air and begin to reach towards the wall (Figure 3).

- Lift your ribs away from your hips and lean to the side until you can possibly touch the wall (Figure 4).

- Turn your palm to face up, and attempt to press it into the wall as you rotate your torso, rib cage, and shoulders (Figure 5).

- Turn your head to look up.

- Firm your leg and buttocks muscles as you press your hands into the wall and rotate more to deepen the pose.

- Repeat the pose on the other side of your body.

Tips for getting into the pose

1. Keep both of your feet on the floor for an easier variation.

2. Press your shoulders down, away from your ears.

3. Lean directly to the side, and avoid collapsing your arms or chest forward.

4. Keep lengthening your lower back by slightly tipping your pelvis under and firming your buttocks.

Exiting the pose

Stand straight, return your foot to the ground, and release your arms to your sides.

Yoga prop suggestions

Place a yoga block between your hands and the wall to ease your reach to the wall.

Suggestions for breathing in the pose

On your inhalations, feel your ribs expanding in all directions like a balloon filling with air. On your exhalations, relax deeply into the side stretch, drawing your navel toward your spine.

Suggestion for visual focus

Let your eyes focus on a point at eye level in front of you at first, and then look toward a point on the ceiling.

Imagery for alignment

Rotate your body from the inside out like a spinning top. Place your attention on your spine and interior torso. Let your shoulders and ribs rotate as a result of a deeper rotation within you.

"Home Play" experiments—exploring and deepening the posture

Turn your head and look toward the ceiling. Point the elbow of your upper arm toward the ceiling as you expand your armpit area. Does this change the experience of the posture?

Now rest your head on the bicep of your bottom arm. How does this change the pose?

If your shoulders hunch, relax them.

Press your palm more - or less - firmly into the wall.

Possible benefits and experiences of the pose

- Promotes openness and expansion in the waist, ribs, and sides of your body.

- Stretches the muscles of the arms and shoulders.

- Strengthens the legs

Precautions

- If your chest and upper body begin to collapse forward, you may be over stretching in this posture.

- Do **not** press your lifted foot into the side of your knee area. Always place your foot above, or below the knee.

Basic Twist Poses At The Wall

Level of difficulty: Beginner

Focus and Intention: Spine, torso, and shoulder stretch

Standing twist variation

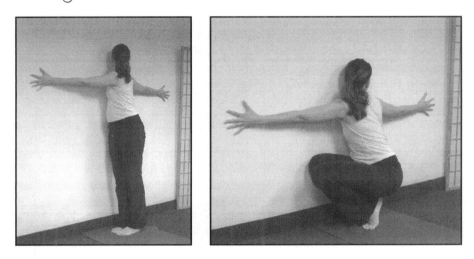

Instructions at a glance

- Stand sideways a few inches from the wall with your feet together and your hip touching.

- Reach your arms out from shoulder height to hug the wall, spreading your fingers (Figure 1).

- Keep your lower body forward by keeping your legs strong and engaged.

- Twist deeply as you turn your head and look behind you.

- Press the center of your chest to the wall.

- Stay in the standing variation, or bend your knees and slide your torso down the wall into a squat. Continue to hug the wall and twist (Figure 2).

- Repeat the pose on the other side of your body.

Tips for getting into the pose

1. You will go further in the twist by keeping your legs, buttocks and abdomen strong and immobile.

2. Keep lengthening your lower back by slightly tipping your pelvis under and firming your buttocks.

3. Reach through your fingertips and extend your arms as much as possible as you twist.

4. Keep your feet and knees together as much as possible.

Exiting the pose

If you are in the squat position, stand up. Release your arms to your sides and turn to face forward.

Yoga prop suggestions

Squeeze a yoga block between your inner knees or upper thighs to cultivate leg strength and alignment.

Suggestions for breathing in the pose

On your inhalations, imagine breathing to the crown of your head as you elongate your spine. Exhale fully, as if your lungs were attempting to touch your spine.

Suggestion for visual focus

Let your eyes focus on a point at eye level behind you or on the thumb of your back hand.

Imagery for alignment

Hug the wall like a long-lost friend. Bring your heart center closer as you soften toward the wall. Feel the support of this solid vertical structure.

"Home Play" experiments—exploring and deepening the posture

Twist ultra slowly, about a half inch or an inch at a time. Initiate the twist from behind your navel. Let the twist then move up into your waist, ribs, shoulders, and finally your neck.

Let your eyes stretch, too. Slide your eyes to their corners in the direction you are twisting.

Explore the relationship between your breath and your ability to twist more deeply into the posture.

Possible benefits and experiences of the pose

- Develops flexibility in the back and muscles surrounding the spinal column.

- Stretches the muscles of the arms and shoulders.

- Strengthens the legs.

- Massages internal organs.

Precautions

- Keep legs engaged and your frontal hip bones pointing forward as much as possible. Avoid over stretching your lower back. Twist primarily from above your navel.

- If you are pregnant, do not twist deeply in the lower body.

- Use caution and consult your doctor if you have back/spinal injuries or have recently had surgery.

Basic twist pose variation—squatting sideways at the wall

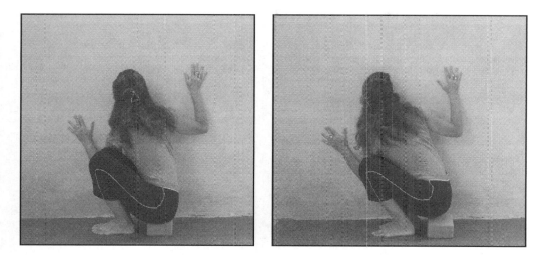

Instructions at a glance

- Place a yoga block on the floor near the wall.

- Squat sideways with your feet together a few inches from the wall until you can sit on the yoga block.

- Turn your body to face the wall.

- Place your elbow on the **outside** of your knee as you begin to twist more deeply (Figure 1).

- Keep your elbows bent and hug the wall.

- For a slight variation, lift off the block and twist deeper, turning to look at the hand behind you (Figure 2).

- Press your elbow into your outer knee.

- Keep your spine erect and chest open.

- Turn to face forward again, stand up, and repeat the pose on the other side of your body.

Basic twist pose variation—seated sideways at the wall

Instructions at a glance

- Sit sideways at the wall with your feet and knees together (Figure 1).

- Your shoulder will touch the wall, but your legs will remain a few inches it.

- Turn your body to face the wall.

- Place your elbow on the **outside** of your knee as you begin to twist more deeply (Figure 2).

- Extend your arm behind you to contact the wall.

- Press your elbow into your outer knee.

- Keep your spine erect and chest open.

- Turn to face forward again, and repeat the pose on the other side of your body.

Seated Spinal Twist Pose At The Wall

Level of difficulty: Beginner/Intermediate

Focus and Intention: Back and spine flexibility. stimulating digestive functions, hip flexibility

Seated spinal twist pose variation—extended leg

Instructions at a glance

• Sit facing away from the wall with one knee bent.

• Your distance from the wall is less than one arm's distance. Your elbow is slightly bent when you place your palm on the wall.

• Place the outside of one of your thighs on the floor allowing the foot of that leg to wrap around the outside of your opposite hip (Figure 1). If this movement is too difficult for you, follow the instructions for the extended leg variation (Figure 5), or one of the other leg variations described in this section.

• Cross your other leg over the bent leg on the floor. You can place the foot to the outside of your knee (Figure 1), or to the inside of your knee for an easier stretch.

• Hug the raised knee firmly with the **opposite** arm (Figure 2).

• With your spine erect, look behind you and turn your torso toward the wall.

• Place your hand about shoulder height on the wall behind you.

• Use the wall to leverage yourself into a deep spinal twist.

• Press your elbow to the **outside** of your raised knee to progress more deeply into the twist (Figure 3).

• Repeat the pose on the other side of your body (Figure 4).

Tips for getting into the pose

1. Keeping your legs and hips stable and immobile will deepen the twist.

2. Lengthen your lower back by slightly tipping your pelvis forward and raising your rib cage.

3. Twist from above the navel, allowing your neck to rotate last.

4. Keep your front foot and both sit bones on the floor.

198

5. Broaden your chest and press your shoulder blades down, away from your ears.

6. Your chin is level with the floor as you turn.

Exiting the pose

Release the twist and face forward. Uncross your legs, and return to a seated position.

Yoga prop suggestions

Sit on a yoga block or a pillow if you have trouble crossing your legs.

Suggestions for breathing in the pose

On your inhalations, grow taller and expand your upper body. On your exhalations, contract your navel and rib cage.

Explore the relationship between your out breath and your ability twist more profoundly, but in a way that feels comfortable and safe.

Suggestion for visual focus

Let your eyes focus on a point at eye level on the wall in back of you, or on the thumb of your back hand.

Allow your eyes to close and go inward to sensation and feeling.

Imagery for alignment

Imagine that you are gently squeezing every drop of stress and tension out of your body as you revolve around the central axis of your body.

"Home Play" experiments—exploring and deepening the posture

Experiment with all these varied arm and leg positions in the twist. Try crossing or uncrossing your legs. Play with hugging your front leg; sometimes loosely, sometimes tightly.

Twist very slowly; about a half inch or an inch at a time. Initiate the twist from behind your navel center. Let the twist then move up into your waist, ribs, shoulders, and finally your neck.

Possible benefits and experiences of the pose

- Promotes openness and expansion in the waist, ribs and sides of your body.

- Stretches the muscles around the spinal column.

- Stretches the muscles of the arms and shoulders.

- Massages internal organs and digestive system

Precautions

- Keep both sit bones in contact with the floor, and twist primarily from the navel upwards to prevent lower back strain.

- Do not twist deeply in the lower body if you are pregnant.

- Use caution and consult your doctor if you have back/spinal injuries or have recently had surgery.

Seated spinal twist pose variation—relaxed legs

Instructions at a glance

- Sit with your back to the wall with your knees bent in front of you.

- Your distance from the wall is less than one arm's distance. Your elbow is slightly bent when you place your palm on the wall at shoulder height.

- Let your knees flop over to one side, and slip your bottom foot under the thigh of the top leg. Cross your arm over to press down on the **outside of your bottom leg** (Figure 1).

- With your spine erect, look behind you and turn your torso toward the wall.

- Place your hand high on the wall behind you (Figure 2), **or** at about shoulder height (Figure 3).

- Use the wall to leverage yourself into a deep spinal twist while keeping your hips close to the floor.

- Press your hand on the **outside** of knee to twist more intensely.

- Repeat the pose on the other side of your body.

Seated spinal twist pose variation—both arms to wall

Instructions at a glance

- Follow the instructions above, sitting closer to the wall.

- Place both hands on the wall for leverage in the twist.

- Move your hips toward the floor.

"Wind Mill" Wide Leg Stretch Pose At The Wall

Level of difficulty: Beginner

Focus and Intention: Leg stretch, back and shoulder stretch, spinal rotation

Instructions at a glance

- Stand a few inches from the wall and place your feet about one leg's length apart, or a distance that is comfortable for you.

- The outside edges of your feet should be parallel to the edges of the yoga mat.

- Hinge forward from your hips and press your sit bones into the wall.

- Place one of your hands onto the floor or on a yoga block in front of you (Figure 1).

- Initiate the twist by placing your other hand behind your head and revolving your torso so that your elbow is pointing toward the ceiling (Figure 1).

- Keep your head and neck aligned with your spine.

- Then, straighten your arm as you reach toward the ceiling behind you (Figure 2).

- Press down on the floor/block and actively turn yourself like a wind mill.

• Repeat the pose on the other side of your body (Figure 3).

Tips for getting into the pose

1. By keeping your legs and hips stable and immobile, you will deepen the twist.

2. Bend your knees slightly if you feel too much tension in your back, or if you find it difficult to twist.

3. Twist from above navel, rotating your neck last.

4. Attempt to keep your sit bones pressing equally into the wall.

5. Broaden your chest and press your shoulder blades down.

6. Your chin is away from your chest in its normal position.

Exiting the pose

Release your top arm to the floor. Step away from the wall, one foot at a time, and return to an upright position. Step your feet together.

Yoga prop suggestions

Place a yoga block or two in front of you, approximately in the middle of your spread legs.

Suggestions for breathing in the pose

On your inhalations, imagine breathing toward the crown of your head. On your exhalations, rotate your ribs, shoulders and neck deeper into the twist.

Suggestion for visual focus

Let your eyes focus on a point at eye level on the ceiling, or on the thumb of your upper hand.

Imagery for alignment

Visualize your body as a wind mill. Your legs are the strong, solid foundation of the structure. Your arms are the blades of the mill. Your neck and spine form the axis from which your arms can turn easily with the wind. As you exhale, imagine the air moving you into rotation.

"Home Play" experiments—exploring and deepening the posture

Try bending your knees more. Notice how the movement alters your ability to twist safely and effectively.

Explore the relationship between your head, neck and spine in this pose. Is your neck collapsing forward, arching back? Allow your spine to elongate as you twist.

Possible benefits and experiences of the pose

- Promotes openness and expansion in the waist, ribs and sides of your body.

- Stretches the muscles around the spinal column.

- Stretches the muscles of the arms and shoulders.

- Stimulates internal organs and digestive system

- Stretches the legs

Precautions

- Keep both sit bones in contact with the wall and twist primarily from above the navel to prevent lower back strain.

- If you are pregnant, do not twist deeply in the lower body.

- Use caution and consult your doctor if you have back/spinal injuries or have recently had surgery.

Standing Forward Fold Pose At The Wall

Level of difficulty: Beginner

Focus and Intention: Hamstring and back stretch, surrender to gravity

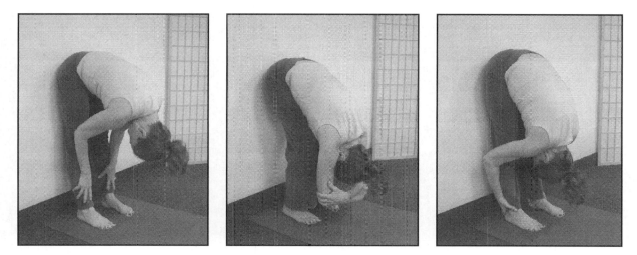

Standing forward fold variation—with blocks

Instructions at a glance

• Stand a few inches or more from the wall with your feet a few inches or more apart.

• The inside edges of your feet are parallel to one another.

• Hinge forward at your hips and press your sit bones against the wall as you put your hands on your shins for support (Figure 1), or on two yoga blocks in front of you (Figure 4).

• Bend your knees so that your stomach rests on your upper thighs, letting your arms dangle overhead, holding opposite elbows (Figure 2).

• Let gravity take you into the stretch as your back and head release toward the Earth.

• To go deeper, straighten your legs and pull your chest closer to your legs (Figure 3).

Tips for getting into the pose

1. Spread your feet farther apart if you are pregnant or your stomach is large.

2. Start with your knees bent. Feel free to bend them even more if you notice any strain in your back or too much tension in the backs of your legs.

3. Attempt to keep your sit bones pressing equally into the wall.

Exiting the pose

Bend your knees and roll up to a standing position— one vertebra at a time.

Yoga prop suggestions

Place two yoga blocks to the sides of your feet or in front of you to support your hands.

Suggestions for breathing in the pose

On your inhalations, feel your body lift slightly. On your exhalations, allow gravity to deepen the pose.

Suggestion for visual focus

Look toward your knees or close your eyes.

Imagery for alignment

Imagine that you are a pair of pants folded over a coat hanger. Let the crease of the fold sharpen as you release into the pose. Feel as if the coat hanger were lifting you up by your hips. Allow your body to dangle loosely like heavy clothing.

"Home Play" experiments—exploring and deepening the posture

Play with bending your knees more and notice the effect on your forward fold. Bend your knees so much that your abdomen - and perhaps your chest - contacts your legs.

Release the tension in your shoulders, upper back, neck, jaw and face.

Move your head up and down, and then side to side as if you were saying "yes," and then "no." Relax your neck with each motion.

Possible benefits and experiences of the pose

- Stretches the muscles of the back and around the spinal column.

- Stimulates internal organs and digestive system.

- Stretches the backs of the legs.

- Increases flexibility and releases tension in the neck.

Precautions

- If you are pregnant, separate your legs to make room for your baby.

- Use caution and consult your doctor if you have back/spinal injuries or have recently had surgery.

- Use caution and consult your doctor if you have high blood pressure, heart problems, or have had recent heart surgery.

Standing Shoulder Stretch "Yoga Mudra" Pose At The Wall

Level of difficulty: Beginner/Intermediate

Focus and Intention: Shoulder and arm stretch

Instructions at a glance

- Stand a few inches from the wall and step your feet a few inches apart or more.

- The inside edges of your feet should be parallel to one another.

- Hinge forward at your hips and press your sit bones into the wall as your arm stretch reach toward the floor (Figure 1).

- Bend your knees so that your stomach rests on your upper thighs, letting your arms dangle, holding opposite elbows (Figure 2).

- Gravity takes you into the stretch as your back and head release toward the Earth.

- Reach your hands behind your back and interlace your fingers, palms facing one another (Figure 4). If your hands cannot clasp, hold the ends of a tie or strap in your hands to bridge the distance (Figure 3).

- Squeeze your shoulder blades together as you reach your hands toward the ceiling.

- Straighten your legs and pull your chest closer to your legs.

• Drop your chin toward your chest and soften your neck.

Tips for getting into the pose

1. Spread your feet farther apart if you are pregnant or if your abdomen is large.

2. Start with your knees bent. Feel free to bend them even more if you feel strain in your back or too much tension in the backs of your legs.

3. Attempt to keep your sit bones pressing equally into the wall.

4. Continue to press your shoulders down away from your ears.

Exiting the pose

Bend your knees as you roll your back up to a standing position. Your head comes up last. Unclasp your hands and let your arms float apart out to your sides. Enjoy the sensations in your arms!

Yoga prop suggestions

Hold a yoga strap or tie between your hands to ease into this deep shoulder stretch.

Suggestions for breathing in the pose

Focus your inhalations into your upper body and shoulders. On your exhalations contract the muscles of your upper back between your shoulder blades.

Suggestion for visual focus

Look at your knees or close your eyes.

Imagery for alignment

Called the "yoga Mudra" in Sanskrit, which means "the symbol (or gesture) of yoga." This posture is classic because we bow our heads (intellect, ego, identity) below our hearts. In my perception, the posture suggests that love is supreme, and reminds us to relinquish our small egos for the sake of returning to the state of yoga—union, connection, oneness.

With this in mind, allow yourself to surrender to your heart, to well-being, and to love. Release whatever negativity you are holding onto mentally and emotionally—even if it is only for a brief moment.

"Home Play" experiments—exploring and deepening the posture

Experiment with the distance between your hands. Try holding a yoga strap even if you think you don't need it. Try pressing your palms together completely. Continue to feel your body and the sensations in your arms before, during and after you release the posture. This pose feels quite blissful when you finish!

Possible benefits and experiences of the pose

- Stretches the muscles of the back and around the spinal column.

- Stretches the chest and strengthens the arms and shoulders.

- Stimulates internal organs and digestive system.

- Stretches the backs of the legs.

- Summons feelings of grace and gratitude.

- Eases shoulder and neck tension.

- Fantastic daily stretch for computer users or those who drive a lot!

Precautions

- Separate your legs if you are pregnant to make room for the baby.

- Use caution and consult your doctor if you have back/spinal injuries or have recently had surgery.

- Use caution and consult your doctor if you have high blood pressure, heart problems, or have had recent heart surgery.

- If you have elbows that hyperextend, maintain a slight bend in your elbows.

Runner's Lunge Pose At The Wall

Level of difficulty: Beginner
Focus and Intention: Leg and hip stretch

Instructions at a glance

- Stand with your back to the wall.

- Take a giant step forward with one foot or stand about one leg's length in front of the wall. Bend your knees and slide your foot backward until your heel reaches the wall.

- Bend your front knee until it is aligned over your ankle.

- Adjust your front foot position until your knee is over your ankle.

- Press the heel of your back foot into the wall with your toes on the floor.

- Straighten and activate your back leg as you keep your frontal hip bones facing forward.

- Place your hands beside your front foot on the floor, or yoga blocks (Figure 1), or near the **inside arch** of your front foot (Figure 2).

- Focus your eyes on a point at eye level in front of you or down to the floor.

- Keep your chest open and spine long.

• Perform the pose with your other leg.

Tips for getting into the pose

1. Actively press your back heel into the wall and straighten your back knee as much as possible.

2. Downward dog is a good transitional pose for entering into the runner's lunge pose.

Exiting the pose

Lean forward to bring your back leg beside the front leg. Return to an upright standing position. Perform the pose with the other leg in the forward position.

Yoga prop suggestions

Place your hands on yoga blocks on the outside or inside of your front foot for support.

Suggestions for breathing in the pose

Breathe deeply into your diaphragm and feel the movement of your breath in your pelvis and hips. As you exhale, relax your hips and sink deeper into the posture.

Suggestion for visual focus

Let your eyes focus on a point on the floor in front of you.

Imagery for alignment

See your front foot anchored to the floor as your back leg extends and presses into the wall behind you. Your body makes a 90° angle to the wall. Your legs, your torso, your arms and your head create a solid form at a right angle to the plaster, wood, stone or drywall behind you. Think of the dependability, reliability and support of the walls in your life, now the same principles apply to you in this posture. Find a balance between the opposite movements in your body; upward, downward, forward and backward.

"Home Play" experiments—exploring and deepening the pose

Without bending your back leg, let your hips melt toward the floor.

Practice strengthening your back leg and then your front leg by squeezing your muscles toward your bones.

Find a balance between relaxing and energizing your legs in the posture.

Notice the sensations in your leg muscles and hips.

Possible benefits and experiences of the pose

- Releases tension in the pelvic region.

- Strengthens and stretches the legs, and lower body.

- Increase flexibility in the groin.

Precautions

For the safety of your knees, point the knee of the front leg in the same direction as your big toe. It should remain directly above or slightly behind your ankle.

Low lunge variation— back knee down

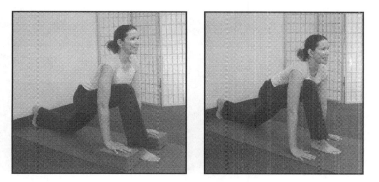

Instructions at a glance

- Follow the instructions for the main posture with your hands on yoga blocks or on the floor.

- Press your foot against the wall as you lower your back knee to the ground.

- Let your knee gently touch the floor; do not put a lot of pressure on your knee cap.

- Align your front knee over your ankle.

• Elongate your spine and look to a point on the floor in front of you.

• Perform the pose on the other leg.

Runner's Low lunge hand variations—finger tips or fists

Instructions at a glance

• Allow your fingertips to support you on yoga blocks or on the floor. This variation lessens the stretch and sensations in your legs and hips (yoga model in the foreground).

• If placing your palms on the floor causes too much discomfort, try making fists then support yourself with your knuckles on blocks or on the floor. Keep your wrists aligned with your forearms (yoga model in the background).

• Continue to press your back foot into the wall.

• Align your front knee over your ankle.

• Elongate your spine and look at a point on the floor in front of you.

• Perform the pose on the other leg.

Runner's high lunge variation—hands on blocks inside the front foot

Instructions at a glance

• This posture is a good option for deeper hip opening, and provides a lunge option for women who are pregnant, large breasted, or anyone whose extra weight is in their mid-section.

• Follow the instructions for the main posture.

• Bring your hands to the **inside arch** of your front foot onto yoga blocks.

• Place your palms flat on yoga blocks at the inside arch of your front foot, or use your fingertips to support you to lessen the sensations in your legs and hips.

• Continue to press your back foot into the wall.

• Align your front knee over your ankle.

• Elongate your spine and look at a point on the floor in front of you.

Pyramid Pose At The Wall

Level of difficulty: Beginner/Intermediate

Focus and Intention: Leg, back, and hip stretch, cultivates balance

Instructions at a glance

- Stand with your back against the wall. Place one heel at about a 45° angle to the wall.

- With your other foot, take a giant step forward.

- Align your front heel with the arch or heel of your back foot.

- Press your back heel into the wall for leverage as you square your hips.

- Hinge forward at your hip crease with your torso parallel to the floor (Figure 1). If your hamstrings tighten, bend your front leg.

- Place your hands on yoga blocks beside your front foot for support (Figure 1).

- Breathe deeply as your torso moves closer to your front leg (Figure 2).

- Gravity takes you into the stretch as your back and head release toward the Earth.

- Hold opposite elbows behind your back to add a shoulder stretch to the posture (Figure 3).

Tips for getting into the pose

1. The distance between your feet should be less than one leg's length apart.

2. Square your hips and engage your legs to make the posture more stable.

3. Start with your front knee bent, and feel free to bend it even more if you feel strain in your back, or too much tension in the backs of your legs.

4. Press your heel into the wall.

Exiting the pose

Place your hands on your hips, inhale, and return your torso to a vertical position. Step your back foot forward and return to a standing position.

Yoga prop suggestions

Place two yoga blocks on either side of your front foot to support your hands.

Suggestions for breathing in the pose

On your inhalations, feel your body lift slightly. On your exhalations, let gravity lower your body toward your front leg.

Suggestion for visual focus

Look at your knee, toes, or close your eyes.

Imagery for alignment

Even if you have never actually seen a pyramid, visualize your best version. Your legs create a solid foundation. Your hips form the apex, the point. As your torso cascades over the smooth slope of the pyramid's vertical incline, try to grasp the perfection in the form.

"Home Play" experiments—exploring and deepening the posture

Attempt to stretch your yoga mat apart with your feet. Then do the opposite; try to scrunch up the middle of your yoga mat with your feet. Notice the effect of this subtle movement on your hip position and ability to balance.

Bend your front knee, releasing your back and torso into the pose. Straighten your legs as much as possible to fire up your quadriceps.

Feel how your experience changes when you alter small aspects of your body's alignment and energy.

Possible benefits and experiences of the pose

- Strengthens the legs.

- Develops balance and steadiness.

- Stretches the muscles of the back and around the spinal column.

- Stimulates internal organs and digestive system.

- Stretches the backs of the legs.

Precautions

- If you are pregnant, take a wider stance when you step your foot forward.

- If you feel off-balance, try the variation with your hands pressing the wall.

Pyramid pose variation—hands pressing the wall

Instructions at a glance

• With your feet together, stand facing the wall.

• Stretch your arms to the wall and place your palms on the wall (if possible at about the height of your navel as in the figure above).

• Take a giant step backward with your back foot turned out at about a 45° angle.

• Align your front heel with your arch or back heel.

• Fold forward - parallel to the floor - as you press your hands into the wall.

• Squeeze your inner thighs together as you turn your frontal hip bones to face the wall.

• If your hamstrings tighten, bend your front knee.

• Activate your arms and back as you push the wall.

• Repeat the pose on your other leg.

Crossed Leg Hip Stretch At The Wall

Level of difficulty: Beginner
Focus and Intention: Leg stretch, hip rotator stretch

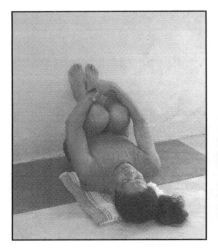 

Instructions at a glance

- With your buttocks against the wall, lie flat on your back. Feel free to use a blanket beneath you for comfort.

- Hug your knees, and push your toes into the wall to bring your knees closer to your torso (Figure 1).

- Straighten one of your legs and rest it on the wall.

- Cross your other ankle just above the knee cap of your straightened leg, and let your hip and knee rotate away from the midline of your body (Figures 2).

- Slowly and gently press your bent knee toward the wall for a deep hip stretch.

- Relax your shoulders and upper body and focus on the sensations in your hips.

- Repeat the pose on the other leg.

Tips for getting into the pose

Keep the foot of your bent leg in a flexed position and avoid letting your ankle twist too much.

Exiting the pose

Uncross your legs, bring your knees toward your chest, roll over onto your side, and return to a seated position.

Yoga prop suggestions

Place a flat blanket under your back for comfort.

Suggestions for breathing in the pose

Breathe deeply into your diaphragm and feel the movement of your breath in your pelvis and hips.

Suggestion for visual focus

Look toward the ceiling or close your eyes and focus inwardly on sensations.

Imagery for alignment

Notice your legs make the shape of an upside down number 4. Allow the center of the four to open and widen as you press your knee out to the side. Establish strong vertical and horizontal lines with your legs like the numeral four.

"Home Play" experiments—exploring and deepening the pose

Focus on the sensations in your hips as you bring your legs closer or push them farther away from your chest. Locate the point of greatest sensation inside your hip area. If it had a color, what color is it? If you were to describe the feeling in one word, what would it be?

Possible benefits and experiences of the pose

- Releases tension in the pelvic region.

- Stretches the legs, knees, and hip rotators.

- Offers relief from long days of sitting in a chair or standing up.

Precautions

For knee safety, do not force your knee away from your chest.

Cross leg hip stretch deeper variation— with leg bent

Instructions at a glance

- Lie on your back on a yoga mat or blanket with your buttocks close to the wall.

- Bend your leg and place one foot on the wall.

- Cross your other ankle just above the kneecap of your bent leg, and let your hip and knee rotate away from the midline of your body (Figure 1).

- To deepen the pose, lift your heel off the wall pressing only with your toes as you bring you legs closer to your chest (Figure 2).

• Slowly and gently press your bent knee toward the wall.

• Relax your shoulders and upper body, and focus on the sensations in your hips.

• Repeat the pose on the other leg.

Leg Cradle Pose At The Wall

Level of difficulty: Beginner

Focus and Intention: Leg, knee, and hip rotator's stretch

Instructions at a glance

NOTE: This posture is similar to the crossed leg hip stretch, except that you are sitting up.

• Sit on the floor or on a blanket, with your back to the wall. Your buttocks and lower back are in contact with the wall.

• Bend your knee toward your chest, and then out to the side. The lower leg is extended (Figure 1), or bent to the side (Figure 2).

• Place your foot into the elbow crease of your opposite arm. If that is not possible, just hold your foot or shin with the opposite arm.

• Grow tall and lengthen your back with the support of the wall as you hug your knee and shin toward your chest.

• Relax your shoulders and upper body and focus on the sensations in your hips.

• Repeat the pose on the other leg.

Tips for getting into the pose

1. Keep the foot of your bent leg flexed, and avoid letting your ankle twist.

2. Lift your chest and upper back.

3. Avoid rounding your shoulders.

Exiting the pose

Uncross your leg and straighten it.

Yoga prop suggestions

Place a flat blanket under your hips for comfort.

Suggestions for breathing in the pose

Breathe deeply into your diaphragm. Feel the movement of your breath in your pelvis and hips. On your inhalation, feel as if you were stretching and growing taller. On your exhalation, draw your leg closer to your chest.

Suggestion for visual focus

Look to a point at eye level in front of you, or close your eyes and focus inwardly on sensations.

Imagery for alignment

Hug your leg toward your heart. Appreciate the support and function of your leg. What would your leg's odometer read if you counted all the miles you've walked or run? Cradle and embrace your leg as you would a baby. Love your leg for however flexible or stiff it happens to be at this moment.

"Home Play" experiments—exploring and deepening the pose

Put all your attention on the sensations in your hips as you dance with your leg.

Slowly rock your leg side to side. Feel what you feel.

Bring your leg closer to your heart or farther from your chest.

Raise your foot higher or lower so that your shin is no longer parallel to the floor.

Using all of these movements, discover the perfect level of sensation for you at this time.

Possible benefits and experiences of the pose

- Releases tension in the pelvic region.

- Stretches the legs, knees, lower back, and hip rotators.

- Offers relief from long days sitting in a chair or standing.

Precautions

For the safety of your knee, do not force your foot toward your chest.

Crane Pose At The Wall

Level of difficulty: Beginner/Intermediate
Focus and Intention: Hamstring and calf stretch

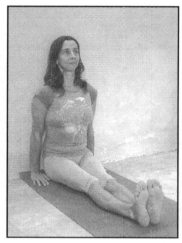 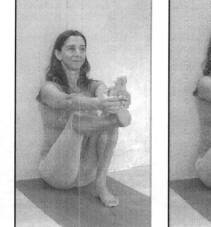  

Instructions at a glance

- Sit on the floor, or on a blanket. With your back to the wall, extend your legs in front of you (Figure 1). Your buttocks and lower back remain in contact with the wall.

- Bend one of your knees toward your chest. Place your supporting foot flat on the floor. If you are unable to do this, extend the supporting leg in front of you.

- Grasp the foot or shin of the leg you will stretch. If you are unable to reach it because of tightness or injury, loop a yoga strap over your foot and grab the ends. Keep your knee slightly bent at first (Figure 2).

- As you breathe, straighten your leg little by little, lifting and pulling it closer to your body (Figures 3 & 4)

- Sit tall and lengthen your back along the wall as you bring your leg toward your torso.

- Relax your shoulders and upper body to focus on the sensations in your hips.

- Repeat the pose on the other leg.

Tips for getting into the pose

1. Flex the foot of the extended leg to deepen the stretch.

2. Lift your chest and upper back.

3. Avoid rounding your shoulders as your hold your leg.

Exiting the pose

Bend your outstretched leg and place it on the floor in front of you. Continue performing more seated poses, or return to a standing position.

Yoga prop suggestions

Place a flat blanket under your hips for comfort.

Wrap a yoga strap around your foot, hold the other ends, and lift your leg up into position.

Suggestions for breathing in the pose

On your inhalation, fill your upper lungs and back. On your exhalation, bring your leg closer to your chest and your navel toward your spine.

Suggestion for visual focus

Look at your knee or toes of the extended leg, or close your eyes and focus inwardly on sensations.

Imagery for alignment

Imagine that your leg muscles are elastic bands slowly stretching to their limit. With every inhalation, the elastic gets longer and longer.

You can also think of your leg as a toggle switch that you flip up and down, on and off. The light is either on or off, depending on the position of your leg relative to your body.

"Home Play" experiments—exploring and deepening the pose

Focus your attention on the sensations in your leg as you bring your leg closer to you a fraction of an inch at a time.

If sensations in your leg become too intense, relax by focusing on your breath, or release your leg away from you again.

Experiment with this posture avoiding force or strain. Give your leg time to let go of tension.

Possible benefits and experiences of the pose

Lengthens and releases tension in the muscles of the back of the leg.

Precautions

- To avoid pulls or muscle strains, **do not** force your leg to your chest.

- If your knees hyperextend, **do not** straighten your leg completely. Always keep a slight bend in your knee.

Quadriceps Stretch Pose At The Wall

Level of difficulty: Intermediate

Focus and Intention: Leg and hip stretch

Instructions at a glance

- Kneel with your back to the wall. Start at about 2 feet from the wall and adjust the distance according to your body's proportions.

- Place your fingertips or hands on the floor beside your front leg for support.

- Slide one of your knees backwards until the top of your foot and your shin touch the wall (Figure 1).

- Lift your other leg forward. Place it on the floor. You may have to help your foot with your nearest hand. Bend your front knee until it is aligned over your ankle (Figure 2).

- Adjust your front foot position until your knee is over your ankle.

- Place your hands on the thigh of your front leg to help lift and straighten your back (Figure 3).

- Move your body closer to the wall depending on your level of leg flexibility.

- This is a very deep quadriceps stretch; please approach it slowly with care. Never force your body!

- Keep your chest open and spine tall.

- Perform the pose on the other leg.

Tips for getting into the pose

1. Press your hands firmly into your thigh and push down into your front foot to deepen the stretch.

2. If sensation is too great with your hands on your thigh, return them to the floor.

3. To avoid pain in your knee, double fold the blanket or yoga mat beneath it.

Exiting the pose

Lean your body forward and place your hands on the floor. Lower your back leg from the wall. Return to a kneeling position.

Yoga prop suggestions

Place your hands on yoga blocks on the outside or inside of your front foot for support.

Place a flat blanket, yoga mat, or thin padding under your knee cap for protection.

Suggestions for breathing in the pose

Breathe deeply into your diaphragm and feel the movement of your breath in your pelvis and hips. As you exhale, relax your hips and legs while you sink deeper into the posture.

Suggestion for visual focus

Let your eyes focus on a point on the floor in front of you.

Imagery for alignment

Imagine that your back leg is a nutcracker, and you want to slowly crack a nut between your lower and upper back leg as you move using your arms to control the amount of pressure.

"Home Play" experiments—exploring and deepening the pose

This posture brings an extreme amount of sensation—well, it does for me!

Concentrate on the feelings in your legs as a meditation as you move closer to the wall. Don't resist, but don't push either. Find a point in the posture where you can remain with equanimity, and continue breathing fully.

Notice how you respond to discomfort. Do you give up quickly, take a warrior's attitude, or move patiently with kindness?

Possible benefits and experiences of the pose

- Releases tension and stiffness in the quadriceps muscles.

- Strengthens and stretches the legs and lower body.

Precautions

- For knee safety and sensitivity, place a blanket or pad under your back knee. The knee of your front leg points in the same direction as your big toe, and remains directly above or slightly behind your ankle.

- Move very slowly into this pose to avoid muscle spasms and cramps in the backs of your legs.

Revolving Head To Knee Fold Pose At The Wall

Level of difficulty: Beginner/Intermediate

Focus and Intention: Side, back, hip, and leg stretch, stimulates internal organs, opens rib cage

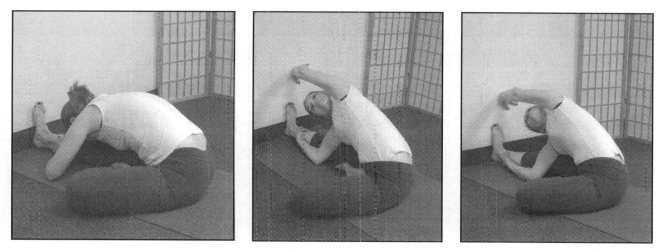

Instructions at a glance

- Sit facing the wall with the sole of your foot pressing flat against the wall.

- Place your other foot on the inside of your outstretched leg; anywhere from the inner knee to inner thigh. Let your knee open to the side.

- If your knee hovers in the air, place a blanket or pillow under your bent knee.

- Lengthen your spine as you hinge forward from your hips toward your outstretched leg.

- As you enter the pose, slightly bend the knee of your outstretched leg. Place your arms - or a yoga support prop - under your knee.

- If you feel flexible, straighten your leg completely.

- Turn your torso to face away from your outstretched leg (Figure 2).

- As you breathe, rotate more and more, opening your armpit toward the ceiling.

- Stretch both of your arms toward the wall. Your hands may touch the wall; if they don't, just continue to breathe and continue to reach.

- As you deepen the pose, you may be able to press your hands into the wall for leverage and turn your head to look up toward the ceiling (Figure 3).

- Reach the crown of your head toward the wall.

- Lengthen the entire side of your body from your hips to your fingertips.

- Repeat the pose on the other leg.

Tips for getting into the pose

1. Pull your shoulders down, away from your ears.

2. Align your neck with your spine.

3. Lean directly to the side with your ear moving toward your knee.

4. Avoid collapsing your arms or chest forward by opening your armpit toward the ceiling.

Exiting the pose

Lift your torso upright, release your arms to your sides, and return to a regular seated position.

Yoga prop suggestions

Sit on the edge of a blanket to help open your hips. Prop your bent knee up with a pillow, blanket, or yoga block.

Suggestions for breathing in the pose

On your inhalations, feel your ribs expanding in all directions like a balloon filling with air. On your exhalations, relax deeply into the side stretch drawing your navel toward your spine.

Suggestion for visual focus

First focus on a point at eye level in front of you and then look toward a point on the ceiling.

Imagery for alignment

Wring your body out like a wet towel. Put your attention on the inside of your torso. Let your shoulders, arms and ribs rotate as a consequence of a deeper revolution inside of you.

"Home Play" experiments—exploring and deepening the posture

If you bend the knee of your outstretched leg, does this help deepen the twist?

Explore the position of your head and neck in relation to the rest of your body when performing the twist. How does your head position aid or hinder the twist?

As you intensify the movement, point your elbow toward the ceiling. Open your armpit. Does this change the experience of the posture?

Now rest your head on the bicep of your bottom arm. How does this change the pose?

If your shoulders hunch, relax and press them down.

Possible benefits and experiences of the pose

- Promotes openness and expansion in the waist, ribs, and sides of your body.

- Stretches the muscles of the arms and shoulders.

- Stretches the legs, hips and back.

Precautions

- Avoid yanking or pulling your body into the twist to prevent strains and cramps.

- If your hips are coming off the floor and your upper body begins to collapse forward, you may be over stretching in this posture. Ease up a bit.

Seated Wide Legs Stretch Pose At The Wall

Level of difficulty: Intermediate/advanced

Focus and Intention: Leg, inner thigh, and hip stretch

Instructions at a glance

- Sit facing the wall.

- Spread your legs comfortably far apart. The arches of your feet are against the wall.

- Press your hands on the floor behind you to push yourself closer to the wall.

- Keep your feet flexed and legs actively engaged.

- When entering the pose, slightly bend your knees. Place a blankets or pillows under your knees for support.

- If you are flexible, straighten your legs, taking care to continue the contraction of your quadriceps.

- Breathe in, and lengthen your spine (Figure 1).

- Breathe out, and relax your torso toward the wall. Bend from your hip/thigh crease, tipping your pelvis forward.

- Holding opposite elbows, let your arms rest on the wall above your head (Figure 2), or partially extend your arms (Figure 3), or fully extend your arms (Figure 4).

- Reach your forehead toward the wall.

- Press yourself closer as you stretch further.

Tips for getting into the pose

1. Move your chest and sternum toward the wall without collapsing and rounding your upper back.

2. Continue to press your shoulders down from your ears.

3. Your arms are relaxed throughout this pose.

Exiting the pose

Push yourself away from the wall, bend your knees, and return to a seated position.

Yoga prop suggestions

Sit on the **edge** of a blanket or pillow to lift your hips and allow your pelvis to tilt slightly forward.

Roll up a blanket or two and place it under your knees to allow the muscles in the backs of your legs to soften and prevent strain in your lower back. If you don't have blankets or pillows, use yoga blocks.

Suggestions for breathing in the pose

As you breathe in, feel the oxygen fill up your chest and expand your rib cage. Feel the breath reach your fingertips. As you exhale, soften your hips and legs and melt into the pose.

Suggestion for visual focus

Close your eyes and experience your body.

Imagery for alignment

Imagine your legs are the hands on a clock. At first, they are at 5 of and 5 after the hour in this posture. No problem, you have time! Perhaps a few moments later you move toward 10 of and 10 after the hour, or the next time you begin the pose. Maybe someday you will open your legs to quarter of and quarter after the hour. Our practice may be timeless, but unlike the hands of a clock, there is limitation in our bodies. At any hour, isn't it amazing how far your body can extend into your space with your legs spread wide? Take a moment to appreciate your legs for wherever they are right NOW.

"Home Play" experiments—exploring and deepening the posture

As you sense you can deepen the pose, return your hands to the floor behind you and nudge yourself a little closer to the wall.

Try flexing your feet more, aiming the balls of your feet and toes toward your head. Notice changes in the sensation in your legs.

Bend your knees a little more or a little less.

Pause and spend some time in the position that feels just right—not too much, not too little sensation.

Tilt your pelvis a little forward toward the wall. If you feel limited in the range of motion of your hips, lower back or pelvis, sit on the edge of a pillow.

Possible benefits and experiences of the pose

- Promotes lower back and hip flexibility.

- Lengthens the hamstrings and inner thighs.

• Enhances awareness of our ability to become more flexible.

Precautions

• Keep your knees bent to prevent lower back strain.

• If you feel an uncomfortable pulling sensation in the insides of your knees, back away from the wall as you could be stretching too far.

• Move slowly and gradually into the pose to prevent muscle strains and soreness.

Standing Wide Leg Stretch Pose At The Wall

Level of difficulty: Beginner
Focus and Intention: Leg and hip stretch

Instructions at a glance

- Stand a few inches from the wall and separate your feet about one leg's length apart, or a comfortable distance.

- The outside edges of your feet are parallel to the edges of the yoga mat.

- Bend your knees slightly, and fold forward from your hip crease as you press your sit bones into the wall.

- Place your hands on the floor, or on yoga blocks in front of you (Figure 1).

- Keep your head and neck aligned with your spine.

- To deepen the pose, hold your ankles or shins and pull yourself under your legs toward the wall (Figure 2).

- Let gravity take you into the stretch as you release your back and head toward the Earth.

- To go deeper, straighten your legs more and draw your chest closer to your legs (Figure 3).

Tips for getting into the pose

1. Start with your knees bent. Feel free to bend them more if you notice strain in your back, or too much tension in the backs of your legs.

2. Press your sit bones equally into the wall.

3. Narrow or widen the distance between your legs appropriately.

4. Press your shoulders down, away from your ears, even though the rest of your back may be relaxing into the pose.

5. Soften your face and jaw.

Exiting the pose

Bend your knees and roll up to a standing position— one vertebra at a time.

Yoga prop suggestions

Place your hands on two yoga blocks in front of you for support.

Suggestions for breathing in the pose

On your inhalations, feel your body lift slightly. On your exhalations, let go more with gravity.

Suggestion for visual focus

Look to a point on the wall behind you, or close your eyes.

Imagery for alignment

Remember the jungle gym at the playground? Imagine yourself draped over the top rung, Lifted by the top rung, your hips are the highest point of the fold. Your hands hold onto your ankles. Allow your upper body to drape loosely and casually over the rung like a child.

"Home Play" experiments—exploring and deepening the posture

Play with bending your knees more, and notice the effect on your ability to fold.

Press into the inside edges, and then the outside edges of your feet. How does this movement effect your hips and legs?

Let go of tension in your spine and back. With every breath, pour everything onto the floor.

Can you let go more, and at the same time maintain good alignment and form in the posture?

Relax your neck as you move your head loosely in the space between your legs.

Does the experience of seeing the world upside down have an effect on you?

Possible benefits and experiences of the pose

- Stretches the muscles of the back and around the spinal column.

- Stimulates internal organs and digestive system.

- Stretches the backs of the legs.

Precautions

- Separate your legs more if you are pregnant.

- Use caution and consult your doctor if you have back/spinal injuries or have recently had surgery.

- Use caution and consult your doctor if you have high blood pressure, heart problems, or have had recent heart surgery.

Plow Pose At The Wall

Level of difficulty: Beginner/Intermediate

Focus and Intention: Lengthening the spinal cord, entire posterior stretch with emphasis on neck and shoulders

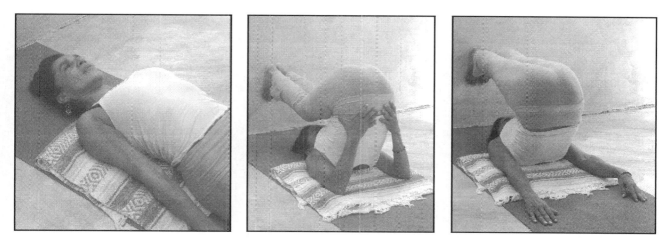

Instructions at a glance

- Place a blanket or two flat on the floor a little over a foot from the wall. Your head is off the edge of the blanket.

- Lie on your back on the blanket with the top of your head about a foot or more away from the wall. Distance may vary based on your body proportions (Figure 1).

- Swing your legs forward and back to gain momentum, and then lift them up in the air over your head.

- Place your hands on your back for support as your feet touch the wall (Figure 2).

- Straighten your legs as much as possible, and release your arms to the floor behind you (Figure 3) or keep them on your back (Figure 2).

- Continue to lift your tailbone toward the ceiling throughout the pose.

- Even though your lungs and diaphragm are compressed by your abdomen, continue to breathe deeply.

243

Tips for getting into the pose

1. Do not move your head or neck while you are in this pose. If you need to move either one, come out of the pose and reposition yourself.

2. Keep your knees slightly bent if you cannot reach the wall, or you feel unhealthy tension in your lower back or legs.

3. Keep your neck aligned with the rest of your spine.

4. Let your chin move away from your chest if you feel pressure in your ears.

5. Lengthen your lower back by moving your pelvis/pubic bone away from your navel.

6. When you release the pose, take time to sense and enjoy the after affects.

Exiting the pose

Place your hands on your back and slowly roll your spine back to the floor.

Yoga prop suggestions

Place a blanket or two under your shoulders and back to create space between your neck and the floor.

Suggestions for breathing in the pose

Make extra effort to keep your breath flowing and deepening, even though your lungs are slightly compressed in this posture.

Suggestion for visual focus

Let your eyes focus on a point on the ceiling or toward your toes.

Imagery for alignment

Remember Silly Putty? First we pulled it into a long roll, and then we folded it over on itself. Your body is body putty, with the ability to extend itself, then fold over itself, and extend itself again. Let your body bend as much as possible in this direction, fully flexing your spine, back, and energizing your nervous system.

"Home Play" experiments—exploring and deepening the posture

Bend your knees more - or less - and notice the effect on the posture

Even though your whole spine is in flexion, how can you keep lengthening your lower back and not collapse in your abdominal muscles?

Extend your time in the pose as you gain experience and flexibility. Work up to 3-5 minutes.

Allow yourself a full few minutes to feel and notice the energy and feelings in your body after you finish plow posture.

Possible benefits and experiences of the pose

- Energizes the whole body and nervous system.

- Stretches the muscles of the neck, shoulders, legs, and back.

- Massages glands of the thyroid and parathyroid in the throat area.

Precautions

- Use caution or consult your doctor if you have high blood pressure or a heart condition.

- Use caution or consult your doctor if you have recently had back surgery, or have spine or disc problems.

- Use flat blankets under your shoulders (not your neck) to prevent neck injuries.

- If you feel too much pressure in your head and face, you may need to limit your time in this posture.

Plow pose variation—one leg up

Instructions at a glance

• After following the instructions for plow posture above, lift one of your legs in the air as you continue to press your foot into the wall.

• Reach actively through the ball of your foot and firm the whole leg.

• Lower that leg, and lift the other in the air.

• Repeat this a few times until you are ready to release the pose.

Pigeon Lunge And Split Poses At The Wall

Level of difficulty: Advanced (use care and common sense)

Focus and Intention: Hip and leg stretch, back bend and chest opener

Instructions at a glance

NOTE: Practice the quadriceps stretch, wheel pose and wall split pose over time to prepare for this advanced pose!

• Kneel on all fours facing away from the wall with your toes touching the wall. Adjust the distance for your body's proportions (Figure 1).

• Slide one of your knees backward until the top of your foot and your shin touch the wall (Figure 2).

• Lift your other leg forward and place your foot on the floor. You may have to help your foot up with the nearest hand. Bend your front knee until it is aligned over your ankle (Figure 3).

• Place your fingertips or hands on the floor beside your front leg for support (Figure 3).

• Adjust your front foot position until your knee is directly over your ankle.

• Place your hands on the thigh of your front leg to help lift your torso. Straighten and arch your back as you move the crown of your head toward the wall (Figure 4 & 5).

• Depending on your flexibility, move your head closer to the wall and your back foot (Figure 5).

• Reach your arms overhead and backwards to place your hands on the wall.

• With an open chest, sink deeply into your hips.

• Locate the toes of your back foot and hold onto them. Your elbows are pointing toward the ceiling.

• Perform the pose on the other leg.

Tips for getting into the pose

1. Dynamically press your hands into your thigh and press into your front foot before proceeding into the back bending aspect of the posture.

2. Warm up your body before attempting this pose.

3. Breathe deeply into your upper chest and back.

4. Getting into this pose can be as challenging as maintaining it: yoga is a process, not a goal.

5. Stop anywhere in the sequence when you have reached your limit.

Exiting the pose

Release your back foot. Lean forward, placing your hands on your thigh, and then onto the floor beside your front foot. Remove your back leg from the wall. Return to a kneeling position.

Yoga prop suggestions

Place your hands on yoga blocks on the outside or inside of your front foot for support.

Place a flat blanket or thin padding under your knee for protection of the knee cap and joint.

Make a loop with a strap or tie to hook over the arch of your foot if you cannot reach it with your hands.

Suggestions for breathing in the pose

Breathe deeply into your diaphragm and feel the movement of your breath beyond your diaphragm into your pelvis and hips. As you exhale, relax your hips and legs to sink deeper into the posture.

Suggestion for visual focus

Let your eyes focus on a point on the wall, or close your eyes.

Imagery for alignment

In the full expression of this posture, your body is creating a complete circle. The crown of your head, the archetypical area symbolizing spirituality is touching your foot, the archetypical area symbolizing the Earth-bound material world. You have come full circle. The polar opposites are connected. Feel the energy cycling through your whole body.

"Home Play" experiments—exploring and deepening the pose

What comes up for you when you see the photos of this pose? If it seems impossible right now, remember that the seedling of a tree contains the potential for the whole tree. Try the first stages of this pose and work into it little by little.

See yourself in this pose in your mind's eye.

As you bend backward toward the wall, breathe deeply and fully into your chest as you open your heart toward the big, vast universe. Expand your lungs, ribs, and throat as much as you can.

Look toward your toes with longing. Reach for them like a long-lost lover.

If you are in the full pose, lift your head slightly, and then lower it slightly without straining your neck. Pull your elbows closer together, then spread them farther apart. Sink deeper into your hips.

Possible benefits and experiences of the pose

- Releases stiffness in the quadriceps muscles.

- Strengthens and stretches the legs, hips and lower body.

- Opens the chest, lungs and rib cage.

- Invigorates the spine and nervous system.

- Bestows confidence and inner strength.

Precautions

- For knee safety and sensitivity, place a blanket or pad under your back knee. Also, the knee of your front leg should be pointing in the same direction as your big toe, and should remain directly above or slightly behind your ankle.

- Move very slowly into this pose to avoid muscle spasms and cramps in the backs of your legs or feet.

- Never force your body into any aspects of this posture.

Pigeon variation—leg split

Instructions at a glance

- Follow the instructions for the beginning stages of pigeon lunge pose.

- Before arching your back, straighten your front leg in front of you and flex your foot (Figure 1).

- Fold forward over the extended front leg (Figure 2).

- While keeping your front foot flexed, slide your front forward into a split (Figure 3).

- You can place pillows or blankets under your front thigh for support if your thigh does not touch the floor (not pictured).

• Place your hands or fingertips on the floor (or on pre-positioned yoga blocks) beside your hips and begin to reach the crown of your head toward the wall behind you (Figures 4 & 5).

• Reach one of your arms over your head to touch the wall or hold your foot (Figure 6).

• Then reach the other arm to hold the same foot as you squeeze your elbows toward each other and toward the ceiling (Figure 7).

• Breathe very deeply into your upper chest as you remain in the pose.

• To exit the pose, release your foot and bring your hands to the floor. Press your hips energetically into the air to order to remove your leg from the extended leg split position. Slide your back knee away from the wall and return to a kneeling position.

• Repeat the pose on the other leg.

Yoga Wall Worksheet

Create Your Own Yoga at Your Wall Sequence

Date:

Sequence Name:

1. Pose Name: Page #:

2. Pose Name: Page #:

3. Pose Name: Page #:

4. Pose Name: Page #:

5. Pose Name: Page #:

6. Pose Name: Page #:

7. Pose Name: Page #:

8. Pose Name: Page #:

9. Pose Name: Page #:

10. Pose Name: Page #:

11. Pose Name: Page #:

12. Pose Name: Page #:

13. Pose Name: Page #:

14. Pose Name: Page #:

Yoga Wall Worksheet

Create Your Own Yoga at Your Wall Sequence

Date:

Sequence Name:

    1. Pose Name: Page #:

    2. Pose Name: Page #:

    3. Pose Name: Page #:

    4. Pose Name: Page #:

    5. Pose Name: Page #:

    6. Pose Name: Page #:

    7. Pose Name: Page #:

    8. Pose Name: Page #:

    9. Pose Name: Page #:

  10. Pose Name: Page #:

  11. Pose Name: Page #:

  12. Pose Name: Page #:

  13. Pose Name: Page #:

  14. Pose Name: Page #:

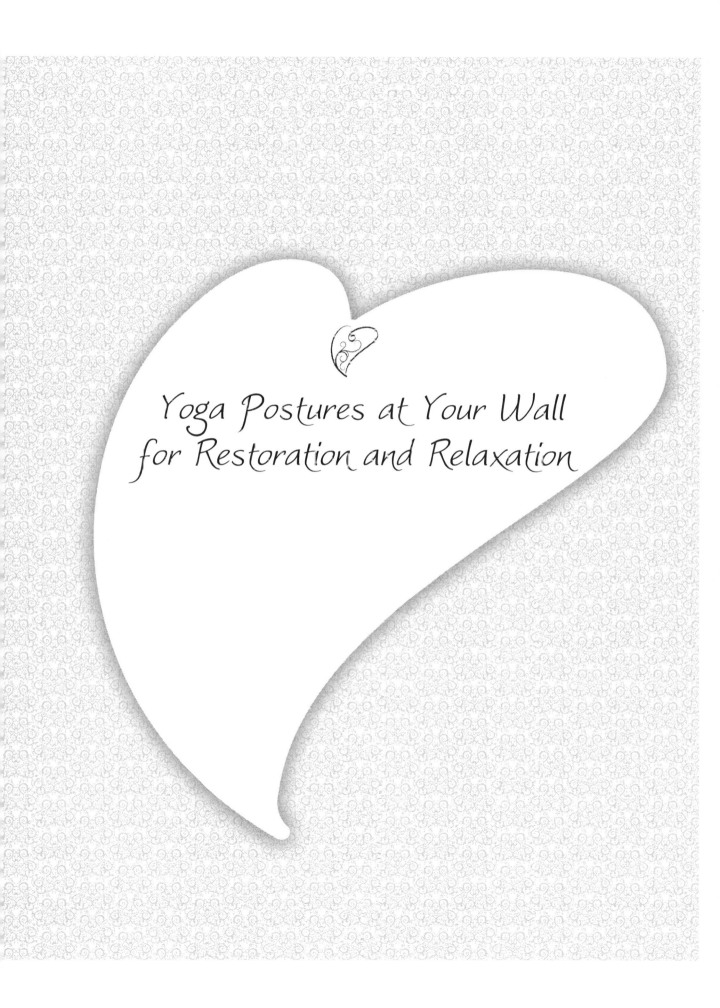

Yoga Postures at Your Wall
for Restoration and Relaxation

Focus on Restoration and Relaxation

When you crave time to be alone, go within, recuperate, chill out, and sink into the stillness of your being, let the wall support your legs. Putting your legs up the wall has an incredible restorative affect on the nervous system, as well as on the feet and legs themselves. If you have never tried it, well, try it! If you are on your feet a lot, these postures offer your feet and legs a respite from carrying all of your body weight.

Some specific tips for practicing the postures in this section:

- If you tell yourself "I can't meditate or relax," or "the relaxing part of yoga is a waste of time," or "I only do yoga to get a work out," then this section is especially for you! You are the one who needs it the most…whether you know it or not. You deserve relaxation. It is your birthright to relax when you need a break.

- To achieve the most benefit, perform any one the postures in the following section for at least 10 minutes. Depending on your needs, you can hold the posture for longer or shorter durations.

- These postures help you to unwind before bedtime.

- If you are not feeling up to practicing the postures in other sections, restorative postures provide benefits to your well-being with little effort.

- Props such as pillows, a blanket, and bolsters will add to your comfort and pleasure in these postures.
- Dimming the lights and playing your favorite music enhances your experience of relaxation. Sometimes you will crave silence.

- Exit the pose slowly, mindful of your renewed relaxation. Don't rush out of the pose unless absolutely necessary.

- Turn off your cell phones and telephones, close the door, and put some time aside to just BE.

Legs Up The Wall

Level of difficulty: Beginner

Focus and Intention: Rejuvenating the nervous system, unwinding, reviving the legs and feet, relaxation

Instructions at a glance

- Sit sideways with your hip to the wall (Figure 1).

- Lean your torso backwards with arms supporting you as you swing your legs up onto the wall, one at a time (Figure 2).

- Lie flat on your back or on a blanket.

- Scoot your hips as close to the wall as possible.

- Relax your arms away from your sides, palms facing up (Figure 3).

- Tilt your chin slightly toward your chest to lengthen your neck and release tension at the base of the skull.

- Take a deep cleansing breath and let go.

- Relax your face, jaw and forehead.

- Remain in this position for 5-20 minutes, breathing naturally and easily.

• Bend your knees toward your chest if your feet begin to fall asleep (Figure 4).

Tips for getting into the pose

1. The closer your fanny is to the wall, creating a 90° angle with your body, the more benefit you will receive from the posture.

2. Have your props set up or nearby before you get into the pose.

3. Put your lower legs on a chair instead of the wall if your feet frequently fall asleep or if you are not able to swing your legs up onto the wall with ease.

Exiting the pose

Lower your knees to your chest. Roll over onto your right side and linger there. Press yourself back up to a seated position.

Yoga prop suggestions

Place a blanket flat under your back.

Place a blanket or pillow under your head.

Place a medium sized sandbag on top of your feet. You can accomplish this by bending your knees and balancing the sandbag on your feet, and then straighten your legs.

Use an eye bag over your eyes. Some eye bags contain therapeutic herbs such as lavender.

Cover yourself with a blanket for extra warmth.

Suggestions for breathing in the pose

Breathe naturally and easily through your nose.

Suggestion for visual focus

Close your eyes.

Imagery for alignment

A complete circle is made up of four right triangles, and your body is making the shape of one of these triangles in this posture. Imagine your body inside this perfect, infinite circle. Relax, soften the hard angles, and release tension in every joint.

"Home Play" experiments—exploring and deepening the posture

Accept yourself for where you are at this time, in this place. Give yourself credit for all that you have been through in your life. Give yourself time to be there with all your thoughts, feelings and sensations. Don't censor anything. Give yourself permission to feel what you are feeling.

Let go of the past, release the future into the future. Anchor yourself in the present moment.

Feel the effects of this pose on your breath and nervous system.

Allow the floor to fully support your body weight.

Feel the places where your body contacts the wall and the floor.

Flatten the small of your back against the floor, which automatically tilts your hips and tightens your abdomen. Then release.

Possible benefits and experiences of the pose

- Promotes restoration.

- Refreshes and relaxes the nervous system.

- Relieves swelling and pressure in the legs and feet.

- Encourages stillness and meditation.

Precautions

- Change your leg position if your feet fall asleep.

- Avoid dizziness by coming out of this pose slowly and gradually.

Legs up variation with blanket under shoulders and back

Legs up crossed leg variation with blanket under head

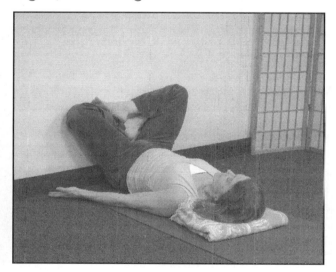

Legs up feet joined variation with blanket under head

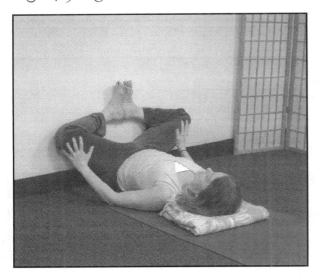

Legs up wide open legs variation with blanket under head

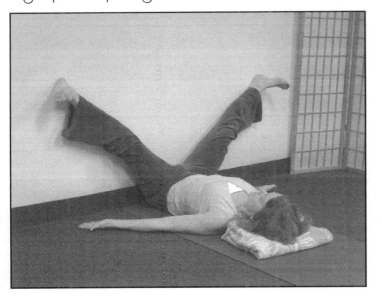

Relaxing On Your Side At The Wall

Level of difficulty: Beginner

Focus and Intention: Transitioning out of restorative and inverted poses, deep relaxation, comfort

 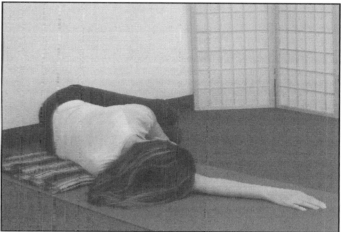

Instructions at a glance

- After finishing inverted postures or supine postures, lie on your side to smoothly transition back to a seated or standing position.

- Let your legs roll over to the right side of your body.

- Move your right arm so that it supports your head; with the elbow bent (Figure 1), or straight (Figure 2).

Precautions

According to the principles of yoga, it is best to lie on your right side after yoga practice, however, it is suggested that pregnant women lie on their left side.

Seated Forward Fold Pose At The Wall

Level of difficulty: Beginner/Intermediate

Focus and Intention: Hamstring and back stretch, focusing inward, releasing stress

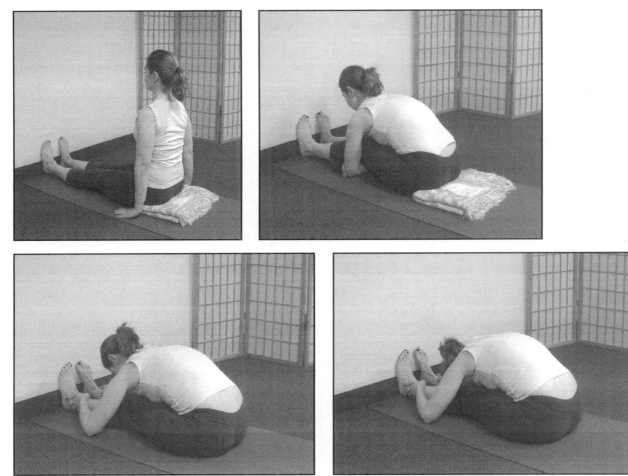

Instructions at a glance

- Sit facing the wall with the soles of your feet parallel to each other and pressing flat against the wall.

- Slightly bend your knees as you enter the pose. You can place your arms or a yoga support prop under your knees (Figure 2).

- If you are flexible, you can straighten your legs completely.

- Breathe in and lengthen your spine (Figure 1).

- Breathe out, and relax your torso forward. Bend from the crease of your hips.

- Reach your hands and arms toward your shins or feet, but do not pull on your feet.

- Let your arms relax to the outsides of your legs (Figure 3 and 4).

- Reach the crown of your head toward the wall.

- Breathe deeply in and out as you elongate your spine forward over your legs.

Tips for getting into the pose

1. Let your breath take you deeper into the pose on your exhalations.
   Never force your body forward.

2. Maintain your chest and sternum moving toward your legs without collapsing and over-rounding your upper back.

3. Keep relaxing your shoulders down away from your ears.

Exiting the pose

Slowly lift your torso away from your legs and return to a seated position.

Yoga prop suggestions

Sit on the edge of a blanket or pillow to lift your hips and allow your pelvis to tilt slightly forward.

Roll up a blanket or two and place it under your knees in order to allow the muscles in the backs of your leg to soften, thus preventing strain in your lower back. If you don't have blankets, wrap your forearms underneath your knees for support (Figure 2).

Suggestions for breathing in the pose

As you breathe in, feel the wave-like motion lifting your upper chest and back. As you exhale, relax and let your body melt into the pose.

265

Suggestion for visual focus

Gaze toward your toes as you begin this pose. As you sink deeper into the pose, you can shift your gaze to your knees or close your eyes altogether.

Imagery for alignment

This pose reminds me of prayer, or acknowledgment of a greater force in the universe. By folding our bodies into a "clothespin" shape, much like two hands coming together in a prayer position, we are physically expressing the inexpressible in a gesture of humility and gratitude.

Hold an image of your own self in this pose in your mind's eye. Visualize yourself going further into the pose without force. See yourself folding deeper and merging with your outstretched legs. See your leg and back muscles elongating.

Maintain an ongoing awareness of the waves of your breath flowing in and out like the pulse of the ocean waves lapping on the shore. Feel the rhythm of the ocean present in your own body.

"Home Play" experiments—exploring and deepening the posture

Try flexing your feet more, bringing the balls of your feet and toes away from the wall. Notice changes in sensation in your ankles and your legs.

Bend your knees a little more or a little less, and spend time in the position that feels just right—not too much, not too little sensation.

Tilt your pelvis a little forward toward your legs.

Relax any tensions in your upper body, neck and face.

Possible benefits and experiences of the pose

- Promotes back and hip flexibility.

- Cultivates relaxation and release of tension.

- Enhances a sense of self-care and nurturing.

- Lengthens the hamstrings muscles in the backs of your legs.

Precautions

- Keep your knees bent to prevent lower back strain.

- Don't pull yourself into the pose; this creates more tension.

- Relax into the pose with your breath to prevent muscle strains and soreness.

"Head to knee" forward fold variation—one leg bent

Instructions at a glance

- Sit facing the wall with the soles of your feet parallel to each other and pressing flat against the wall.

- Place one foot on the inside of your outstretched leg; anywhere from the inner knee to inner thigh. Let your knee open out to the side.

- Place a blanket or pillow under your bent knee if it is hovering uncomfortably in the air.

- Slightly bend the knee of your outstretched leg; at least as you enter the pose. You can place your arms or a yoga support prop under your knee.

- If you are flexible, you can straighten your leg completely.

- Relax your torso forward over your outstretched leg. Bend from the crease of your hips.

• Reach your hands and arms toward your shins or feet, but do not pull on your feet or toes.

• As you go deeper into the pose you may be able to press your hands into the wall (Figures 2 and 3).

• Reach the crown of your head toward the wall.

• Breathe deeply as you elongate your spine and soften into the forward bend.

• Return to a seated position and repeat the pose on the other leg.

Reclining Spinal Twist Pose At The Wall

Level of difficulty: Beginner

Focus and Intention: Back and shoulder flexibility, massaging internal organs, unwinding tension

Instructions at a glance

- Lie flat on your back with your knees bent and feet on the wall.

- Shimmy and wiggle your hips closer to the wall.

- Press your feet flat against the wall and walk them down to the floor on one side of you.

- Stack your knees and feet on top of one another.

- Stretch your arms out into a "T" position at shoulder height.

- Allow your shoulders to relax flat on the floor as much as possible.

- Slowly but firmly, press your knees down with the hand that is closest to them.

- Turn your head and neck to look in the opposite direction from your knees to achieve a full spinal twist.

- If turning your neck feels too uncomfortable, keep your head centered and look at the ceiling.

- Walk your feet over to the other side and perform the pose.

- Roll over onto the right side of your body and rest after you have finished performing the posture on both sides (Figure 3).

Tips for getting into the pose

1. Let your breath take you deeper into the pose on your exhalations.

2. If your shoulder rises off the floor during your twist, walk your feet up the wall a bit so that your legs are slightly off the floor.

3. Let your shoulders settle down into the floor.

Exiting the pose

Roll over onto your right side after you have finished performing the posture on both sides. Press yourself up into a seated position.

Yoga prop suggestions

Place a folded blanket or pillow under your legs/knees for a less intense twist, or if you find your shoulder rising up off the floor.

Place a blanket flat under your back or head for added comfort and relaxation.

Place the blanket flat under your back and shoulders before performing the pose.

Suggestions for breathing in the pose

As you breathe in, feel your spine getting longer. As you exhale, twist yourself deeper into the pose.

Suggestion for visual focus

Gaze toward the wall or floor in the direction you are facing. Look to the ceiling if your head is in a centered position.

Close your eyes to enjoy a more inward experience of the posture.

Imagery for alignment

With each exhalation, imagine any tensions getting squeezed out of your body like water being wrung out of a wet towel. Bring your focus to the inside of your body and your spinal column.

"Home Play" experiments—exploring and deepening the posture

Bend your knees a little more or a little less as you move your hips closer or farther from the wall. Spend time in the position that feels just right—not too much, not too little sensation.

Turn your neck more as if you were trying to listen more closely to the floor. Imagine you can hear the wood, stone or fabric whispering to you.

Possible benefits and experiences of the pose

- Promotes back, neck and hip flexibility.

- Releases tension in the back, spine and shoulders.

- Stimulates internal organs.

- Cools down the body after a vigorous yoga practice.

Precautions

- Use props for support if you have spine or disc problems.

- If you have recently had spinal surgery you may want to skip this posture. Ask your doctor.

- Relax into the pose with your breath to prevent muscle strains and pulls.

Child's Pose At The Wall

Level of difficulty: Beginner

Focus and Intention: Hip, leg, and arm stretch, relaxation, retreating inward, calming your nervous system

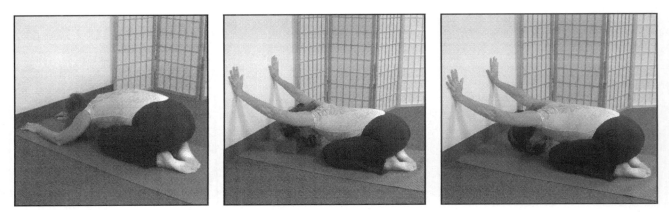

Instructions at a glance

- Facing the wall, kneel 2 to 3 feet away from the wall (depends on your arm length), and sit backward onto your heels.

- If this is not accessible to you, try using yoga props.

- Bring your knees and big toes together. If you have tight legs and hips, separate your knees.

- Roll your torso down over your legs and extend your arms to the wall (Figure 1).

- Walk your hands up the wall and press your palms into the wall.

- Straighten your arms and move your shoulders away from your ears.

- Let your head relax toward the floor or on a yoga block (Figure 2).

- Breathe deeply and relax your spine forward over your legs.

Tips for getting into the pose

1. Relax your face and neck.

2. Keep moving your shoulders down, away from your ears.

3. Move yourself closer to the wall if your palms can't press fully onto the wall.

Exiting the pose

Release your hands from the wall. Roll your spine up to an erect position. As you roll up slowly, think of a string of pearls rising from a jewelry box. Swing your legs to the front of you, and return to a seated position.

Yoga prop suggestions

Put a blanket or pillow between your hips and feet if there a space between them when you are kneeling.

Place a blanket flat under your knees and tops of your feet to avoid discomfort as your bones press into the floor.

Place a pillow or yoga block under your forehead to increase neck safety and comfort.

Suggestions for breathing in the pose

As you breathe in, follow your breath up into your shoulders, arms and fingers. Feel your spine rising, and breathe all the way down into your lower back. As you exhale, release all the air from your lungs, and enjoy the relaxation as you surrender forward and inward.

Suggestion for visual focus

Close your eyes for this pose. Go inward, become quiet and be still.

Imagery for alignment

Imagine that you are a turtle crawling back into its shell. Allow yourself to feel protected, nurtured, and safe as you retreat inward.

"Home Play" experiments—exploring and deepening the posture

For a more active stretch in your shoulders and hips, increase the pressure from your hands onto the wall. Your hips will nudge your heels down.

Separate your knees more and let your stomach release toward the floor. Notice changes in the overall feeling of the pose.

Relax any tension in your neck and face.

Extend the time you spend in the pose, especially after a hectic or stressful day or a vigorous yoga practice.

Possible benefits and experiences of the pose

- Promotes back, leg and hip flexibility.

- Cultivates relaxation and release of tension.

- Enhances a sense of self-care and nurturing.

Precautions

- If you find that knee or ankle injuries prevent you from doing this pose, practice the seated forward fold pose instead.

- Avoid dizziness by coming out of this pose slowly and gradually.

Yoga Wall Worksheet

Create Your Own Yoga at Your Wall Sequence

Date:

Sequence Name:

     1. Pose Name: Page #:

     2. Pose Name: Page #:

     3. Pose Name: Page #:

     4. Pose Name: Page #:

     5. Pose Name: Page #:

     6. Pose Name: Page #:

     7. Pose Name: Page #:

     8. Pose Name: Page #:

     9. Pose Name: Page #:

     10. Pose Name: Page #:

     11. Pose Name: Page #:

     12. Pose Name: Page #:

     13. Pose Name: Page #:

     14. Pose Name: Page #:

After the Wall: the Wash, the Wonder, and the Wide Open Window —W.O.W.!

Life is the same...and different now that I have finished writing *Yoga at Your Wall.*

I still need to do my wash. I still wonder every day about why I am here, and what I should be doing.

There is still the daily challenge of remembering to keep my windows open when I feel like closing the doors, and accepting the walls I meet, instead of hitting them.

The experience of writing this book through stressful times was cathartic and inspiring. It gave me confidence that I can manage to write and practice yoga—even when the rug is pulled out from under me. Even when it feels like the wind wants to blow me down the dirt road and into the sewer system, I can redirect my energy. I can rely on my yoga wall for support, enjoyment, and "re-collection."

What comes next? Who knows? Mystery, and more unfolding mystery. I have no desire to hide from the bitter-sweet flavors of love and longing, knowing and not knowing, being on the Earth and simultaneously moving forward toward dissolution, transition, and rebirth. It is inevitable. It is the truth in this "land of opposites."

Enough for now.

On to my next book, *Reflections of a Codependent Yogi: Exploring the Stickiness of Relationships and the Longing for Self-Love.*

That should keep me busy!

Namaste,
Stephanie Pappas
January 2009

About the Author

Stephanie (a.k.a. Stefani) Ann Pappas has been practicing and teaching yoga since 1992, and is an experienced registered 500 hour level yoga teacher with Yoga Alliance. Stephanie began directing yoga teacher trainings in 1999. In 2002, she founded the Devalila Yoga Teacher Training program, a registered 200 hour level training, and has certified over 150 teachers. She is also a massage therapist and ethnic dance instructor.

Stephanie currently teaches classes, workshops, and yoga teacher trainings in the U.S.A. and Mexico. Stephanie is the co-author of 9 other books on yoga, in addition to her last solo book, *Yoga Posture Adjustments and Assisting*.

Contact Stephanie to teach workshops or training at your studio. She loves to travel!

You can contact Stephanie at stefanipappas@hotmail.com or visit her web sites:

www.DevalilaYoga.com

www.YogaPostureAdjustments.com

www.YogaAtYourWall.com

www.CodependentYogi.com

www.CasaPastel.com

Visit my blog: stefyoga.wordpress.com

Visit my Facebook friends and business pages: Stephanie Pappas, stefanipappas@hotmail.com

About the Photographic Models

From left to right, top to bottom, Devalila Yoga Teacher Graduates 2008: Paula Pablo, Pauline Gyllenhammer, Charlotte Avallone, Kim Karsh, Jacqueline (Jacki) Olsen.

Paula Pablo teaches yoga in the Metuchen of NJ. Contact her at paula_pa@yahoo.com

Pauline Gyllenhammer teaches yoga in the Hillsborough area of NJ, and is also a great massage therapist. Contact her at pgyllenhammer@yahoo.com

Charlotte Avallone teaches yoga, Pilates, and body sculpting in the Bridgewater area of NJ. Contact her at charlotteavallone@msn.com

Kim Karsh is a cert_fied and registered yoga teacher and personal trainer in Hunterdon County, NJ. Contact her at kimkarshfitness@gmail.com

Jacqueline Olsen is a teacher of the handicapped in NJ, a certified yoga teacher, and Reiki practitioner.

Manuel Cano Diaz is a jewelry designer and silversmith in Tulum, Mexico. Manuel also teaches salsa and flamenco classes. Visit his web site: www.ManuelCano.com

Laura Rodriquez is a yoga practitioner and professional chef working in the NYC area.

Silvia Revuelta lives in Tulum, Mexico where she teaches public and private yoga classes. Contact her at niccloxx@yahoo.es

Erin Kipe-Klemme teaches Vinyasa yoga in NJ. Contact her at erin.yoga@me.com

Maria Guadalupe Diaz Alcantara teaches yoga in Tulum, Mexico. She is a professional flamenco dancer and teacher for over 20 years. Contact her at olelamaria@hotmail.com

Other Books by Stephanie Pappas

Yoga Posture Adjustments and Assisting:
An Insightful Guide for Yoga Teachers and Students
Trafford Publishing, 2006, ISBN 1-4120-5162-2,
ISBN-13 978-1-4120-5162-0

Reflections of a Codependent Yogi
Exploring the Stickiness of Relationships and the Longing for Self-Love
Trafford Publishing, to be released in 2009, ISBN 1-4251-2116-0,
ISBN-13 978-1-4251-2116-7

ISBN 142517213-X

9 781425 172138

Made in the USA
Lexington, KY
26 May 2014